Aspects of modern sociology

Social research

GENERAL EDITORS

John Barron Mays
Eleanor Rathbone Professor of Sociology, University of Liverpool

Maurice Craft
Senior Lecturer in Education, University of Exeter

Sociology in Britain—A Survey of Research (1969), by Dr. Krausz
Ethnic Minorities in Britain (1971), by Dr. Krausz

Social Research Design

Ernest Krausz, M.Sc.(Econ.), Ph.D.

Reader in Sociology
The City University

and

Stephen H. Miller, B.Sc., Ph.D.

Lecturer in Psychology
The City University

Longman

Longman
1724-1974

LONGMAN GROUP LIMITED
London and
Longman Inc., New York

Associated companies, branches and representatives throughout the world

© Longman Group Limited 1974

First published 1974

ISBN 0 582 48763.6 cased
           48764.1 paper
Library of Congress Catalog Card Number 73–86127

*Set by Libra Press Limited
and printed in Hong Kong
by Dai Nippon Printing Co. (HK) Ltd.*

Contents

Editors' Preface

The first series in Longman's *Aspects of modern sociology* library was concerned with the social structure of modern Britain, and was intended for students following professional and other courses in universities, polytechnics, colleges of education, and elsewhere in further and higher education, as well as for those members of a wider public wishing to pursue an interest in the nature and structure of British society.

This further series sets out to examine the history, aims, techniques and limitations of social research, and it is hoped that it will be of interest to the same readership. It will seek to offer an informative but not uncritical introduction to some of the methodologies of social science.

JOHN BARRON MAYS
MAURICE CRAFT

Foreword

It will become apparent to the reader of this introductory text that psychology and sociology serve here as basic sources for the explanation of social science methodology. To be sure, as we shall see in the chapters that follow, each discipline leans more heavily on one of the methodological approaches discussed in the book: psychology on experiments and sociology on field surveys. There is a common interest, however, which permeates the text throughout; namely, a desire to achieve greater accuracy in the measurement of social and behavioural phenomena, and an attempt to strengthen the social sciences by means of objective research. This does not necessarily mean that the social scientist must become a statistician. But it does mean that he should understand statistical concepts and be numerate as well as literate. We have, however, avoided statistical formulae and computations, although we have assumed an interest in and understanding of statistical concepts.

It is still the case in much social research that those undertaking the work often embark on it with neither sufficient preparation nor having weighed up alternative possibilities. Much data is gathered without the necessary planning and forethought as to how exactly it will enable the researcher to provide the explanations he is seeking in his topic. Even less thought is usually given to measurement reliability and validity. Methodologists are often approached, too late, at the analysis stage and then have the onerous task of informing the researcher that much of his material is next to useless.

In order to avoid this we have reviewed here at a fairly elementary level the main ideas and steps with which every social scientist should familiarise himself in order to be able to design his research. The *raison d'être* of this text is the propagation of the notion that there is a need for care in the design of even seemingly simple kinds of investigation in the social sciences.

More specifically the book's functions are to outline the basic procedures of research design and to alert the reader to the consequences of adopting different procedures. The book also points the way to more advanced sources, and it should, therefore, be suitable for undergraduate and postgraduate students just beginning their research projects, as well as for the professional social scientists in universities, research units and government departments who are relative newcomers to the enterprise of social research.

Our modest attempt to present the essentials of social research design has been greatly helped by the valuable comments we have received from Professor C. D. Harbury, Head of the Department of Social Science and Humanities, The City University, London, and from Professor A. B. Cherns, Department of Social Sciences and Economics, Loughborough University of Technology.

Empiricism in the social sciences

Empirical research in the social sciences has of late come under severe attack from several quarters. One of the centres of criticism contains mainly ideologists who see the study of human history and human behaviour as a fertile ground for the propagation of certain political viewpoints and for whom the idea of neutrality is anathema. Neutrality and objectivity are, however, basic premisses which guide the activities of most social scientists in their day-to-day research work. We shall dismiss this kind of criticism as being at best irrelevant to *scientific* social research, and at worst damaging so far as substantive work in the social sciences is concerned.

There can be little doubt that some of the views questioning the scientific nature of the social sciences are tantamount to a plea for the use of intuition and introspection as the main tools of social research. We argue that reliance on purely subjective sources of evidence represents an extreme antiscientific stance which would in the end destroy the whole *raison d'être* of the social sciences.

From yet another quarter come more serious criticisms which have been put forward both by natural scientists and by some scholars in the social sciences themselves. They claim that the methodology adopted by the social sciences is broadly similar to that used in the natural sciences, whereas the very nature of the material studied in social science is fundamentally different from that investigated by the natural scientist. The atom, they say, cannot think as the human being can; and there is no question of free will or individualism in the physical world as there is in the human one. Consequently different research strategies would be required to unravel the nature of social phenomena.

This argument depends on the validity of the distinction between human and physical events. We shall not discuss this matter in detail here but simply point out that many philosophers and social scientists do not accept the distinction, or do not regard it as pertinent to the type of methodology used in social research. For example, Alfred Schütz has dealt with such criticisms sympathetically but nevertheless has this to say:

> most of these highly generalized statements (regarding the differences) are untenable under closer examination and this for several reasons. Some proponents of the characterised arguments had a rather erroneous concept of the methods of the natural sciences. Others were inclined to identify the methodological situation in one particular social science with the method of the social sciences in general. Because history has to deal with unique and nonrecurrent events, it was contended that all social sciences are restricted to singular assertory propositions. Because experiments are hardly possible in cultural anthropology, the fact was ignored that social psychologists can successfully use laboratory experiments at least to a certain extent. Finally, and this is the most important point, these arguments disregard the fact that a set of rules for scientific procedure is equally valid for all empirical sciences whether they deal with objects of nature or with human affairs. Here and there, the principles of controlled inference and verification by fellow scientists and the theoretical ideals of unity, simplicity, universality and precision prevail.[1]

Another group, not animated by ideological considerations, question nonetheless the feasibility of ever attaining true objectivity, which is a basic assumption among positivist social scientists. This, they say, is because complete detachment is unattainable in a field which deals with subjective aspects of social phenomena. That complete detachment is not possible where we have to choose between a number of topics for investigation is undeniable. This must be the main plank on which those fighting for social responsibility in science must operate, but this in itself cannot question the need for objectivity in the operational aspects of research.

More generally it is a truism that neither social science nor any other science or intellectual enterprise operates in a vacuum. Their purity is to that extent questionable. The effect of the *Zeitgeist,* of the given language, of the accumulation of human history cannot be eliminated, and Karl Mannheim's reservations on this score remain.[2] But to impugn our ability to think objectively and to suggest that the unconscious, impulsive, irrational factors are the real basic determinants of all knowledge is unacceptable.

Our position may, therefore, be summed up as one which regards the social research procedure as a scientific enterprise. By this we mean a striving after objectively derived facts about the real world, and the systematic organisation of these facts into general explanations (theories) of social behaviour. At the same time we would wish to make the qualifying statements, that *(a)* certain scientific methods of research are not equally applicable to the physical and social sciences, nor are those developed in the social sciences equally useful in all the disciplines; *(b)* some disciplines have achieved greater scientific refinement and depth than others, so that in a *de facto* sense some are more scientific than others.

So far we have attempted to give a brief but clear indication as to our basic approach to social research. Such an orientation is necessary in that it will influence the design of research in many ways. It will ultimately determine not only the techniques employed e.g. of measurement, experiment, observation, etc., but also what kind of models and concepts will be used and how the existing theories will be applied and new ones developed.

CONCEPTS, MODELS AND PARADIGMS

The researcher in the social sciences does not have a completely free hand when he starts his project. He will have at his disposal the results of some research which may be relevant to his own intended investigation. His study may be a replication of previous research in which case he has a great deal to draw on. But even if there are no directly relevant *empirical* findings there will almost certainly be a range of theoretical concepts about the topic of interest. These existing ideas will interact with the researcher's own theories and will to some extent influence the course of the

3

investigation. Broadly speaking we may distinguish three levels of theoretical content—the concept, model and paradigm—each of which may serve as vehicles for the influence of past theorisation on the present.

In this section we shall define these terms, illustrate their meaning with examples, and consider their implications for the design of research.

Concepts are abstract ideas which are used to classify together things sharing one or more common properties. Hence, 'man', 'heavy' and 'round' are all concepts since they serve to delineate things, or properties of things, which have something in common. Where a concept has been deliberately invented for some scientific purpose, for example the use of 'socio-economic status' by a sociologist, the term *construct* is sometimes employed instead of *concept;* the distinction is far from clear and in this text we use both terms interchangeably.

Concepts are, of course, the basic elements of theory. They are, in a sense, the mental units which the researcher manipulates and redefines as he attempts to build explanatory models of the social world. But because concepts are abstract we have to find some empirical correlate capable of being measured if we are to evaluate our theoretical model. The process of choosing observable indicators of our concepts is a major problem for the social researcher (see chapter 2). Even a fairly simple concept such as 'unemployment' requires a careful selection of indices for its measurement. When we come across a more complex concept as for instance 'social mobility' the tracing of indicators becomes an arduous task. It is clear that besides more obvious criteria such as occupation, income, consumption level, leisure pattern, and so on, there are other more subtle and elusive aspects involved in the form of political attitudes, educational goals, interest in neighbourhood, etc. In other words the use of concepts should enable us to focus with greater clarity on relevant aspects of a problem, while their careful application in empirical research will force us to look for the most adequate indicators or indices in order to carry out effective measurement and analysis.

4

Another heuristic tool is the *model,* which may be regarded as the conceptual framework which one employs when conducting a study or empirical investigation. When the researcher begins his work he will often approach the area of human behaviour or the social or economic problem he is investigating from a certain angle, which will immediately give some order or coherence to his material at hand.[3] Any one model relates concepts in a particular way. Thus the same concepts may be related differently in another model. For example in sociology a pluralistic model of society would emphasise the divisiveness and conflict aspects of social life within which a study of relationships between deprived minorities and dominant élitist groups can fit. But equally the concepts of minority group and élite would enter into an integrationist model of society where the stress would be put on the different functions of such groups within an overall unified social system.

The model simplifies or reifies the reality and as such it does not exactly correspond to it—it is isomorphic with some of the important features of reality. The advantage in the use of a model is, however, that it provides a rough first approximation of actual behaviour and enables the researcher to grasp the fundamentals of a problem without having to deal with it in all its complexity from the outset. He can subsequently add the complexities and come nearer to reality. The danger is that the researcher may forget the abstracted nature of his model and therefore regard reality and the area he is researching from an unrealistic point of view. Another drawback is that if the researcher introduces the model too soon, i.e. at too early a stage, this will restrict the range of both theoretical and operational possibilities still open for his design. Thus the researcher would be ill-advised to adopt a particular model before he has thoroughly acquainted himself with the background of the topic he wishes to study. Only after a survey of the available qualitative material and after careful trial tests and pilot studies will he be in a position to judge how suitable a model is likely to prove in his research field.

Finally, one's design will be influenced also by certain very general assumptions known as *paradigms.* Paradigms may be regarded in the Kuhnian sense as world views which affect the orientations of both physical and social scientists.[4] According to Kuhn there are shifts in the paradigms scientists use and in this sense the paradigm must be regarded as the scientist's prevailing fashion. Much of economic analysis, it may be said, is bounded by the paradigm of rationality in economic affairs—the idea of 'the economic man'. The underlying premise in economic analysis, and for that matter in sociological analysis, could on the other hand be the Marxist thesis that it is 'the relations of production', in particular the question of the ownership of the means of production, which fundamentally determines the processes of human behaviour, whether in the economic, social, political and even psychological aspects. A basic paradigm in individual psychology is that of viewing man as an information processing channel.

The question may be raised as to the effects paradigms have on the progress made in research. They constitute *a priori* assumptions for the researcher which tend to shape his general approach and subsequent choice of models or concepts, possibly even the choice of his research techniques. Paradigms in this Kuhnian sense are indeed, as he argues,[5] maintainers of the *status quo* in scientific work—as such they could prove to be restraining influences and they could stifle novel departures and experimentations with new ideas which are the very essence of scientific research.

Although paradigms tend to be rigid there are circumstances in which they may change. There exist, however, even more basic notions which serve to define the structure of the social sciences. For instance economic analysis is based on the fact that there is a scarcity of goods. Psychology rests on the recognition of the systematic organisation of human behaviour. The sociologist's work would become meaningless without the acceptance of certain universal features of social life, that is the interrelationship and interdependence of individuals in groups. These fundamental properties determine the very existence of the social sciences and the subdivisions within them.

The heuristic aids we have considered may be seen as the elements in the explanatory system used in research. Thus, concepts may be looked upon as the simplest elements, models more complex structures, and paradigms the more holistic notions. Paradigms imperceptibly keep one's research within certain confines which enhance the comparability and additiveness of results. Models, on the other hand, are crucial for setting forth the overall plan or pattern for the analysis of the relationships among the variables which the investigator may discover. Conceptualisation facilitates the choice of indicators and their evaluation; giving us, therefore the ground level prerequisites of research.

SEARCHING FOR WHAT?

The design the researcher will adopt for his investigation will depend in large measure on the purposes of the research project. One may pursue a research goal which would result in purely descriptive data, in fact-gathering of the simplest kind. Providing straightforward demographic data for a country would comprise research of this nature. In the chapter dealing with the design of surveys the discussion will turn on the steps involved in some of the problems encountered in this kind of research.

Another more important pursuit of the social scientist is to establish any connections that may exist between several sets of facts, which in turn may lead to certain theories regarding human behaviour possibly with predictive value. In other words, the ultimate goal of the social scientist is to *explain* human behaviour in its various facets. Explanation will involve *causal analysis*, that is uncovering factors that cause certain trends or effects.

Our contention about the ultimate goal of the social scientist necessitates a brief statement regarding the account given by philosophers of science as to the order and logic whereby the researcher can attempt to achieve such a goal. This order and logic is summarised in the title: the *hypothetico-deductive method*. This means that from a general hypothesis and particular statements about initial conditions, which at least for the time being are accepted as true, a predictive statement is deduced.[6] The hypothesis by its very nature, however, is speculative, and its correspondence

7

with observable reality is open to doubt. It is at this point that empirical observation is involved to test the hypothesis. If the prediction turns out to be true the hypothesis is supported, thus contributing to the development of explanatory theories.

Hypotheses may be of a broad nature, emanating from background studies, and enabling the researcher to focus on a certain area. In sociology such a broad hypothesis would be for instance that 'there were likely to be differences in the social relations within families of different sizes';[7] in economics that 'changes in income bring about changes in the amounts saved'.[8] Many hypotheses are more specific, an example from American research in social psychology being that 'the superior northern environment has an effect in raising the intelligence test scores of southern-born Negro children'.[9] Where the researcher is attempting to design an exploratory study in a field as yet little examined, he may start off without any hypotheses, his aim being in fact to produce them. At best a vague type of hypothesis may fulfil his requirement. In more thoroughly studied areas he will have to formulate his hypotheses more clearly and to make them as specific as possible, otherwise his contribution to the field may prove sterile.

Not all hypotheses will be testable to the same extent. Verification will usually, and falsification will sometimes, be incomplete. One reason for this is that some of the variables,[10] such as type of housing, level of education, income, making up the environment of northern-born and southern-born children in the kind of hypothesis mentioned above, may be difficult to control or to measure accurately. Another reason is the intrusion of outside factors. For example in the case of the income-savings hypothesis there may be international economic influences affecting the decisions to save certain proportions of one's income. Such problems are unlikely to arise in the case of the testing of hypotheses experimentally in laboratory conditions, a method used with a good deal of success by psychologists (see chapter 4).

The difficulties in controlling variables or in accounting for all relevant variables does not invalidate a search for covariances and temporal sequences.[11] Neither does it stop us from claiming that certain things do not merely coexist or do not merely succeed one another, but that they are linked in a causal fashion.[12] As we shall see in a later chapter some designs of research will need to be complex in order to discuss the way in which numerous variables are linked and how they affect one another. The problems in this area are daunting, but although they do not destroy the feasibility of hypothesis testing and arriving at causal explanations in the social sciences, the difficulties have produced the situation that social scientists have as yet hardly ever arrived at fully tested or confirmed scientific laws. On the other hand they have been able to produce through scientific methods plausible causal explanations and large numbers of statements of association with varying degrees of probability. Where some phenomena have been found 'constantly associated over a wide range of situations the claim of a causal nexus between them is strengthened'.[13] An example given by MacIver is the constant association between economic depression and a decrease in the number of marriages. We still cannot conclude that under all social conditions economic depression and a decrease of marriage rate go together, but we can claim that given a certain type of socio-economic organisation, the onset of a depression acts as a check on the marriage rate.[14] Once certain regularities of this kind are validated we are enabled to construct theories which will give us a fuller understanding of the relationship between the phenomena in question.

In fact the task of the social scientist is twofold: to test and support existing hypotheses or theories and to generate new hypotheses and construct new theories. Specific theories, whether newly formed or existing ones modified, must be seen, therefore, as emerging from research. It is true that research is guided by existing theory and that it takes place within the paradigms or basic assumptions made in the discipline. But we must also recognise that as Merton says:

> the clarification of concepts, commonly considered a province peculiar to the theorist, is a frequent result of empirical research. Research sensitive to its own needs cannot easily escape this pressure for conceptual clarification. For a basic requirement of research is

that the concepts, the variables, be defined with sufficient clarity to enable the research to proceed, a requirement easily and unwittingly not met in the kind of discursive exposition which is often miscalled 'sociological theory'.[15]

Theories which are grounded in empirical research are crucial in that they enable the social scientist to explain, rather than just describe, human behaviour and social phenomena. It is the discovery of regularities in human life which has made causal explanation possible. Logically this ought to make predictions also possible, for explanation and prediction are part of the same process, and the very regularities discovered may provide the basis for prediction. Perhaps the simplest example may be taken from those aspects of human life which exhibit cyclical trends.[16] The life cycle itself enables demographers to make population projections and a cyclical element may be seen in class imitation which could enable us to predict fashions and attitudes in a society. It is true that the cycles could be disturbed by sudden changes such as war affecting birth rates, and the consequences of such an event on population growth. The length of a cycle and the rate of diffusion in the case of class imitation could also vary a great deal. In the case of business cycles government control may be introduced, although some knowledge of the latter could itself be helpful in arriving at predictions.[17] But if prediction in the social sciences is precarious so it often is in the natural sciences. The biologist cannot predict which of the qualities of the parents will be inherited and the seismologist cannot tell us what earthquakes will occur.[18] Despite this, the seeking of prediction as well as of explanation of past known events is what all empirical scientists engage in.

It is easier to design a piece of research which will seek only to explain what has already happened, for in such an instance we are more certain about the variables we have to take into account. Hypothesis testing itself is a process which involves prediction, but it simplifies this process, particularly in experimental work, in that it specifies the conditions under which a certain outcome will be expected. Similarly if one specified the conditions in which a theory purports to forecast the course of future events, the theory is less likely to be falsified; its usefulness would, however, be diminished. One of the difficulties encountered in social science is that the research procedure itself as well as the predictions made may influence future human behaviour. Thus, since the famous Hawthorne experiments, social scientists have been very conscious of the dangers of influencing the subjects they study by the very process of social research. One of the major functions of research design is to insulate the behaviour under study from the contaminating effects of the research process.

Our aim in this short manual is to introduce the researcher to the various designs he can resort to according to his interests, the dictates of the subject matter and the conditions under which he is to undertake his investigation. In the first instance we discuss the possibilities open to him so far as measurement techniques are concerned. Subsequently we focus our attention on designs with differing degrees of control: fieldwork, especially where surveys are used by sociologists; the analysis of documentary material which may be undertaken in all the social sciences; and experimental research, particularly as used by psychologists in the laboratory situation.

Measurement 2

Perhaps the most fundamental problem in the methodology of social research is how to go about measuring the variables that enter into theoretical statements. The measurement process is in fact the only bridge between these statements and the empirical observations on which they are based, so that without adequate measurement procedures the theories themselves become untestable. Many unresolved disputes in the social sciences, for example the dubious status of psychoanalytic theory, can be traced back to the problem of being unable to measure the theoretically significant variables. It is therefore essential at the outset of our discussion of research design to consider the measurement problems the researcher will have to face. We must emphasise that our aim is not to survey specific techniques[1] but rather to alert the reader to the underlying assumptions of measurement and to outline the important criteria for deciding between alternative methods.

Let us begin by considering briefly the task of a research psychologist wishing to test the hypothesis that frustration leads to aggression. It can be seen that there are two aspects to this problem: first, he must select observations which are related to frustration and aggression, and second, he must try to show that the presence of frustration in an individual is likely to lead to aggression. In formal terms he needs (1) to devise empirical measures of the variables contained in the hypothesis and (2) to find a strategy for revealing the causal connections between them.

In practice it is rarely possible to separate these two research functions completely; the choice of measurement techniques invariably influences the method used to test the relationships expressed in the hypothesis. However for the time being the distinction will be maintained. In this chapter we shall consider the measurement process itself, and move on to the related question of research design in chapters 3 and 4.

THE IDEA OF MEASUREMENT

In everyday life the measurement of physical variables like length or weight is taken for granted. The procedures followed are usually familiar to us and do not raise any conceptual problems. In the social sciences we are concerned with more complex measures, such as intelligence or anxiety, or group attributes such as mobility, power and cohesiveness. Although these variables are more difficult to measure than simple physical quantities the fundamental principles of measurement are the same. At the level of definitions the same procedures are involved.

Essentially the measurement process consists of assigning numbers to objects in accordance with the extent to which they possess a specified attribute or feature. It is not the object itself which is being measured but an *attribute* of the object, for example its length, weight or intelligence. In the social sciences the 'objects' are normally individuals or groups of individuals and the 'attributes' are more often social-psychological than physical in nature. But the definition of measurement is still satisfied provided *numbers are being used to represent how much of an attribute is present in an object.* According to this definition the measurement of intelligence using an IQ test and the measurement of a length using a carefully calibrated ruler are equally legitimate examples of measurement. The problem for the social scientists is not in achieving measurement *per se,* but in achieving *good* measurement in the sense of meaningful, unambiguous representations of the required attributes.

When a physical attribute is being measured it is easy to agree on the *rules* for representing the amount of the attribute in numerical terms. Instruments are available to assign numbers to different lengths in a fixed and precise manner, and scientists will generally agree that the set of numbers obtained embodies in some real sense the relations between the lengths of the objects measured. In the social sciences the position is different. There is often no intuitively obvious connection between the measurement procedure and the variable being measured. There are no psychological rulers with which to measure intelligence, nor are there sociological scales in which to weigh discrimination. It is true that carefully constructed questionnaires and tests have been devised in the social sciences, but the rules they embody are less obvious, and more difficult to apply consistently, than the corresponding rules for physical measurement. The result is that there is always some uncertainty in moving from the level of empirical measurement to the level of theoretical constructs. As we shall see certain technical procedures enable us to minimise this uncertainty but it can never be totally eliminated.

OPERATIONALISM IN THE SOCIAL SCIENCES

This gap between empirical measures and theoretically defined variables is reflected in the terminology used in measurement. Whereas the physical scientist refers directly to the measurement of length or weight, the social scientist talks of measuring *indicators* of his theoretical variables rather than the variables themselves. Thus, the salary a student expects after graduation may be used as an indicator of his ambition. The number of reasoning problems a student gets right in a particular test may be taken to represent his intelligence. And the amount of sweat generated by a student prior to sitting an examination may be used as an index of his anxiety. In each of these cases we are not measuring the psychological properties directly, but instead observable aspects of behaviour which are presumed to be indicators of these underlying properties.

This state of affairs poses fundamental problems for social science research. If we cannot measure social variables directly how do we know that the indicators with which we work really do reflect the variables they are supposed to? An even more fundamental question is whether these underlying variables serve any useful scientific purpose given that they can never be directly measured or observed?

The operationalist position championed by the physicist Bridgman[2] and extended to the social sciences by Lundberg,[3] Stevens[4] and others is quite explicit on this question. Such writers point out that the ultimate goal of science, and the criterion on which it is to be judged, is its capacity to predict the relationships between carefully defined *observable* measures. This being the case we are only complicating matters by regarding our measures as 'indicators' of something else, of hypothetical variables of which we can have no direct knowledge. According to this view the social scientist— and indeed any scientist—should concern himself solely with the relationships between variables defined *operationally;* i.e. by the observable procedures used in measurement. It is all right to study the relationship between sweating rate and scores in an IQ test, but misleading to interpret one's findings in terms of the relationship between anxiety and intelligence, unless of course these words are used in the restricted sense of 'what sweating rate measures' and 'what an IQ test measures'. As Blalock[5] points out the essence of the operationalist argument is that variables are defined by the operations used in measurement and that without an operational definition a variable has no scientific meaning.

It is easy to understand the attractions of the operationalist position. Few social scientists would disagree with the premise that ultimately any test of a scientific hypothesis must depend upon demonstrable relations between operationally defined measures. If nothing else the operationalists have performed a service in emphasising the need for testable theories whose predications link up with something that can be objectively perceived and measured. Kerlinger puts this point well:

Scientific investigators must sooner or later face the necessity of measuring the variables of the relations they are studying. . . . The importance of operational definitions cannot be overemphasized. They are indispensable ingredients of scientific research because they enable researchers to measure variables and because they are bridges between the theory-hypothesis-construct level and the level of observation. There can be no scientific research without observations, and observations are impossible without clear and specific instructions on what and how to observe. Operational definitions are such instructions.[6]

The operationalist, of course, goes one step further than this since he dismisses theoretical constructs altogether, except as labels for operationally defined events. Hence he avoids any embarrassment when theoretically connected tests, for example two IQ tests, produce markedly different results. Since each test defines its own attribute or construct there is no *a priori* reason why the two sets of operations should lead to the same set of measurements.

Despite the simplicity and convenience of the operationalist viewpoint few social scientists would accept it completely. The scientific costs may already have occurred to the reader. First, in the strictly operational system there is no incentive to modify or improve existing measurement techniques. Since there are no theoretically defined concepts, there are no intuitive criteria for modifying tests which fail to produce fruitful correlations with each other. The tendency will therefore be either to retain useless measures and thereby inhibit the flexible development of a science, or to add a new construct for every minor modification of a measurement procedure. As Waters and Pennington say: 'The slightest change in any aspect of a set of operations would mean, therefore, a new concept and would demand, likewise, a new symbol for its designation. A multiplicity of concepts could scarcely be avoided'.[7]

A second and related point is that operationalism tends to inhibit the development of theoretical generalisations capable of unifying a range of specific findings and results. The reason for this is that in an operationalist system the important variables and constructs are never defined in terms of theoretical interrelationships or 'meanings', but in terms of operations alone. Hence there is no basis for generalisation, nor for intuitive insight into the possible relationships underlying perceived events. As Northrop[8] has pointed out even such carefully controlled studies as the Wilson cloud chamber experiment in physics would be totally incomprehensible without some purely theoretical notions about electrons, and it need hardly be remarked that in the social sciences concepts like creativity, social mobility and discrimination are extended far beyond their operational definitions for the purpose of improving measurement procedures and developing new theoretical propositions.

In summary then, we have adopted the position that theoretical constructs must be associated with operational measures if the predicted relationships between them are to be scientifically tested. At the same time we would not regard such operational measures as anything more than indications of the underlying variables themselves. To treat operations as anything more than this, for example as the sole criteria of meaning, would result in a far too restrictive and inflexible approach to the research process. In the section which follows we shall begin to see the implications of this viewpoint for the way in which measurement techniques are developed and evaluated.

WHAT IS A GOOD MEASUREMENT TECHNIQUE?

There are two basic requirements of any form of scientific measurement. First, the measuring instrument must produce consistent or dependable results in the sense that a particular 'object' will receive the same rating if it is measured a number of times in identical conditions. The term *reliability* refers to the degree of consistency present in a measuring instrument. It is obviously high for physical measurement procedures like weighing or measuring length with properly calibrated instruments. In such situations the rules for assigning numbers to objects are quite explicit and unambiguous and there is little room for error or variability to creep into the results. In the social sciences it is more difficult to achieve high reliability in measurement. In the field of attitude measurement, for example, there is always the possibility that respondents may misunderstand the statements they are required to evaluate, or equally the interviewer or test scorer may misinterpret the respondents' verbal reactions. Such chance factors will inevitably lower the reliability of the test, and it is unlikely that exactly the same set of attitude ratings would be obtained if the same respondents were retested. Low reliability is therefore a form of inaccuracy caused by the sensitivity of the measuring instrument to factors which vary randomly from one measurement situation to another. The objective when developing measurement techniques is therefore to keep the influence of random factors to a minimum and thereby preserve the accuracy of the instrument to measure whatever it measures. Reliability is therefore a consequence of a measuring instrument's accuracy.

But accuracy in measuring what? There is not much point in measuring something accurately if it is not the variable we originally intended to measure. So the second requirement of good measurement technique is that it should measure what it is supposed to measure and not something else. This property is known as *validity*.

A measuring instrument can be perfectly reliable without being valid, but the converse does not apply. Suppose, for example, an eccentric researcher suggested that the length of a person's nose was a good index of social mobility. The measures obtained would be highly reliable in the sense that repeated measures of the same set of noses would yield almost identical results. But the measures would still be invalid because it is extremely unlikely that nose length has any relationship to changes in occupational status. Nose length would therefore be a reliable but invalid measure of social mobility. On the other hand it is impossible to devise any measure which is unreliable and yet valid. An unreliable test, by definition, is not measuring anything, so it cannot possibly be valid.

ASSESSING RELIABILITY

Reliability is normally assessed by calculating the agreement between two applications of a measuring instrument on the same set of people. The *correlation coefficient* between the two sets of measures represents the numerical index of reproducibility for that particular measurement technique. When used in this context the correlation coefficient is normally called a *reliability coefficient* and it assumes values between 0 (no reliability) and 1 (perfect reliability)—the two sets of measures are in perfect agreement.

Of course many measurement procedures cannot be assessed in this way because the application of the first test may influence an individual's performance when the measure is repeated. For example in a test of mental ability individuals may remember their responses from one occasion to the next and this will result in a spuriously high correlation between the two sets of results. The straightforward test-retest method of assessing reliability is therefore not satisfactory for many forms of social measurement, and alternative procedures are adopted. One common method is to administer two parallel forms of the same instrument to a set of individuals and to take the correlation between the two sets of scores as an estimate of the correlation between two applications of a single test. Another approach is to divide a measuring instrument into two equivalent halves, in which case the reliability will be some function of the correlation between the scores from the two halves.

The details of these procedures, and the statistical theory on which they are based, are technical matters beyond the scope of this book.[9] However certain general conclusions are important for the proper understanding of the principles of research design. The main point is that reliability is an essential prerequisite of any worthwhile social research, and adequate steps should be taken to ensure the reliability of the measurement techniques used in any particular study. Unless this is done one may be faced with data that is unreliable and largely determined by chance fluctuations in one's measurement procedure. If the variables contained in a hypothesis cannot be reliably measured the relations between them will certainly not emerge, however sophisticated the research design is in other respects. Furthermore if a measuring instrument's reliability is unknown, the researcher will be unable to interpret any failure to obtain the predicted relationships between his measures. He will not know whether his original hypothesis was at fault or whether his measurement techniques were too inaccurate and unreliable for the true relationships to emerge. In short the whole exercise will have been scientifically futile.

In practice the assessment of an instrument's reliability need not be too time-consuming. Most psychological tests of ability, personality and attitude have been carefully investigated by their authors and the reliability coefficients have been determined empirically, often on a very large sample of individuals. Provided the test is to be used on a group of people broadly similar to those used by the author in computing the reliability coefficient there will be no need to make a fresh assessment of reliability. However if a reliability coefficient has been computed for a group in which there was a wide range of performance (for example a random sample of male adults) and the test is now to be used with a more homogeneous group (for example medical students), the established reliability coefficient will be deceptively high and a correction should be made.[10]

It should also be noted that some of the measurement techniques used in social research embody such simple and unambiguous measurement rules that the possibility of chance factors disrupting the process is extremely remote. This is true, for example, of many socio-economic variables such as length of education or marital status, which can be assessed quite accurately from the records of government agencies, and from national census data. Also physical variables such as height, weight or sex, which sometimes enter into demographic research, do not pose any serious measurement problems. Finally certain behavioural measures such as human reaction time, error rates, visual thresholds and so on, can be measured in psychological laboratories with a high degree of accuracy. In such cases, although an occasional error may occur, the overall reliability of the data is intuitively obvious and need hardly be supported empirically. Hence it is only when the researcher wishes to develop a new technique which does not embody simple measurement rules, that the reliability must be empirically determined by one of the methods referred to above.

The required level of reliability depends, of course, on the general nature and purpose of the research and it would be meaningless to specify a value for the reliability coefficient which would be considered satisfactory for all purposes. For correlational research (see chapter 3) where the aim is to demonstrate the quantitative relationships between variables, and for experimental designs (see chapter 4) where one examines the effects of manipulating one variable on another, a reliability of about 0.80 is normally considered satisfactory. At this level 80 per cent of the variation in one's measurements is caused by real differences between the individuals being measured, and only 20 per cent is due to random errors in the measurement process. Beyond this level of reliability the statistical significance of one's research findings (i.e. the clarity with which hypothesised relationships emerge) will not be markedly improved by increases in measurement reliability. On the other hand if a measurement procedure is being used to classify individuals for some practical purpose, e.g. the selection of University students on the basis of IQ scores, a higher reliability will normally be required.

ASSESSING VALIDITY

The achievement of high reliability in measurement is a necessary condition of worthwhile research, but it is no guarantee of success. As we have already shown, for research findings to be meaningful the measures used must possess validity as well as reliability. Not only must they measure something accurately, but the 'something' must correspond to what the researcher thinks he is measuring. Although validity cannot be achieved without reliability, by itself reliability is of little consequence. Our imaginary student of social mobility is a case in point: as long as he measures this variable in terms of 'nose length' his progress will be strictly limited, and this despite the high reliability of his chosen measurement technique.

The achievement of validity then is what really matters in social research. It is much more than a technical prerequisite of good

35622

research. It is more like a bridge between theory and research, and as we shall see the achievement of validity is intricately bound up with the whole research process, and not something which can be treated separately, and in advance, as is the case with reliability.

In a previous section we discussed—and rejected—the operationalist notion that science should concern itself exclusively with observable measures and the relations between them. Instead we argued that scientists needed to *think* in terms of theoretical constructs but to use operational measures of these constructs for the purposes of empirical research. For example, one might theorise about 'status' as though it were 'position on a prestige hierarchy' but measure it in terms of an individual's income and length of education.

The cost of theorising in one language and conducting research in another is that ultimately one must demonstrate the connection between the two. One has to show that income and length of education really do reflect status, and not something else. The problem has no simple answer for the obvious reason that the underlying variable cannot be directly measured by any independent technique. How, then, is one to test the validity of such indirect measures?

The approach normally adopted is to make a number of predictions about how the measure ought to behave if it really were valid and then to test these predictions empirically. Suppose, for example, our theoretical ideas on status suggest that it will be positively correlated with self-esteem and authoritarianism, negatively correlated with sociability and unrelated to other personality characteristics like extraversion and neuroticism. These are essentially social-psychological predications based on a theory about how status influences an individual's behaviour and self-perception. We might also consider the sociological significance of status and predict, for example, that the groupings we observe in society tend to be fairly homogeneous with regard to status; freemasons are normally middle-class, pigeon fanciers are often working-class, and so forth. These various predictions can now be tested empirically using our operational measure of status. If the predictions are confirmed, our theory about status is supported and, at the same time, our operational measure of status is validated. The measure is said to possess *construct validity* because it behaves like the theoretical construct it is supposed to represent. If the predictions are not confirmed we must conclude either that the theory is incorrect, or that the measure is invalid, or both. In this case one might decide to reformulate the theory, or modify the measurement technique depending on the nature of the empirical results and their relations to other results.

The logic behind construct validity is therefore quite straightforward. First, define the variable to be measured in theoretical terms, that is in terms of its relationships with other theoretical constructs. Second, elaborate a series of logical predictions from the theory. Third, test the predictions empirically using the operational measure whose validity is in question. So long as the results agree with the predictions, construct validity has been demonstrated, and also the theory in which the construct is embedded has been supported. In this sense the assessment of construct validity is coextensive with the whole process of scientific research.

This combined process of hypothesis testing and measurement validation is not always as simple as this summary may suggest. In the first place it is not often that only one of the variables in the predicted network of relationships is of uncertain validity. More frequently a number of constructs will lack valid operational measures. But it is also common for some measures to be valid indicators of two or more underlying variables; for example, examination performance may reflect intelligence, motivation and writing speed. The correlation between two such 'multiple indicators' then becomes extremely difficult to interpret. Finally some of the variables in the theory may not be measurable at all, serving only to mediate the relations between other variables which can be measured. In these circumstances the researcher must be quite explicit about the theoretical relationships he is predicting, and the presumed connection between the theoretical variables and the operational measures. If his predictions are then confirmed they may be used to support the main theory as well as the auxiliary theory relating measures to constructs. The simplest form of auxiliary theory is one in which only one measure requires validation, and when the measure may be assumed to represent a single underlying variable. This was the case in the example above concerning the validity of a measure of status. However the same principles apply where more complex auxiliary theories are involved.[11]

It should be noted however that this procedure does not provide logically conclusive evidence for the truth or falsity of the main and auxiliary theories. Even if the empirical findings are as predicted it is always possible that another pair of theories could have predicted the same outcome, so that the results of a single study are at best only supportive. In practice construct validity is only achieved when a series of interlocking studies sharing elements of the main and auxiliary theories all produce consistent results in a variety of different research settings. In addition it is sometimes possible to investigate the auxiliary theory independently of the main theoretical statements. Suppose, for example, that the main theory contains the variables 'status' and 'intelligence' embedded in a network of hypothesised relationships, and that the auxiliary theory specifies the relations between these constructs and operational measures as follows:

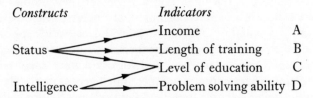

Constructs	*Indicators*	
	Income	A
Status	Length of training	B
	Level of education	C
Intelligence	Problem solving ability	D

We can now make a partial test of the auxiliary theory before studying the main theory which includes these constructs. This can be done by examining the inter-correlations between a group's scores on each of the indicators specified in the auxiliary theory. In the case above we would expect high correlations between *A, B* and *C,* and also between *C* and *D,* but near zero correlations between *A* and *D,* and between *B* and *D.* If this pattern of correlations were obtained it would suggest that there is a common factor underlying *ABC* and a separate factor underlying *CD,* thereby supporting the auxiliary theory. This is, in fact, a very simple presentation of a sophisticated statistical technique known as *factor analysis*[12] which can be used as a tool for establishing construct validity by mapping out the basic constructs or factors which seem to underlie sets of correlated measures. For our present purpose we should note that the technique of factor analysis may provide evidence for the auxiliary theory over and above that obtained by testing the predictions of the main and auxiliary theories in combination. These two lines of approach therefore provide converging evidence of construct validity.

The foregoing discussion describes the procedure for validating a measure for which there is no external criterion of the attribute being measured. It sometimes happens however that a researcher may wish to develop a new measurement technique for a variable he can measure perfectly well in another way. For example a psychologist may wish to replace a rather lengthy test of intelligence with a shorter, more convenient measure of the same variable. In this case the validity of the new test is expressed quite simply as the correlation between the existing and the new measures; the higher the correlation coefficient, known here as a *validity coefficient,* the better the agreement between the test and the accepted criterion. Essentially the same logic is involved in assessing the validity of a measure which will be used to predict some aspect of future behaviour. Thus one may wish to be able to predict final degree performance on the basis of a written test administered to first year university students. Here again there is no difficulty in obtaining a criterion measure (the final degree result) but we require a predictor of that criterion. These two types of validity are known respectively as *concurrent* and *predictive* validity. They are clearly of limited significance in social research as they can only be used in situations where a valid measure of a theoretical construct has already been developed. The important issue in most scientific research however is to bridge the gap between constructs and operational measures rather than to predict one operational measure from another. Hence predictive and concurrent validity have more relevance to the solution of applied problems such as selecting personnel, or developing simpler measurement techniques for use by non-specialists, than to the advancement of scientific understanding.

MEASUREMENT AND RESEARCH DESIGN

Measurement is not an end in itself, but a means of capturing in quantitative form aspects of reality which can be used to support or falsify our theories about social behaviour. In the preceding sections we have outlined the main features required of measurements which are to serve this function of hypothesis testing, but we must also recognise that the actual measurement procedures adopted in any study will have implications for the way in which the testing is done. In other words we cannot consider measurement problems independently of the whole process of research design. In this final section we shall briefly consider some of the interactions between measurement techniques and research design.

Perhaps the fundamental issue concerns the distinction between the two broad classes of design which we have labelled *experimental* and *correlational* in the chapters which follow. In a correlation design all the variables entering into the hypothesis have to be measured, whereas in the experimental design at least one variable is actively manipulated rather than being measured. Hence the choice of measurement techniques will be partly determined by the choice of research design. To take a simple example the hypothesis that frustration leads to aggression might feasibly be tested in two ways; either we could *induce* frustration in some experimental subjects and *measure* the change in their aggressiveness, or we could *measure* the levels of frustration and aggression present in a sample of individuals and test for a correlation between the two variables. Both strategies might lead to a confirmation of the hypothesis but each would require different types of measurement. In the experimental study frustration would not be measured at all, but rather the operations necessary to induce frustration would have to be defined, while aggression would be measured on the basis of observations of aggressive behaviour. In the correlational study it is more likely that frustration and aggression would both be measured using more indirect devices such as questionnaires or projective tests designed to assess an individual's general level or position on these two dimensions. Leaving aside the relative merits of these two strategies of research, the point we wish to make is that fairly detailed consideration of design has to precede the most basic measurement decision—whether to develop an operational definition of a variable for the purpose of manipulation or measurement?

Let us now assume that the appropriate measurement techniques have been selected for use in a particular research study. According to our earlier definition of measurement we should obtain from our measurement procedures a series of numbers which will represent the extent to which an attribute is present in our subjects, or sample groups. Now these numbers which are obtained according to the rules of measurement are also part of the formal, analytic number system which we use in many situations and which has its own properties. Thus we generally accept without question that the difference between 6 and 4 is the same as the difference between 4 and 2 (equal intervals) and that 6 divided by 3 is the same as 10 divided by 5 (equal ratios). But these properties of the number system are not necessarily present in the empirical phenomena which are being measured. For example, it would be nonsense to suggest that the difference in ability between a student who obtained 2nd place in an examination and one who obtained 4th place was the same as the difference between the students placed 4th and 6th. Clearly the measurements obtained by this procedure do not possess the property of equal intervals. Equally one could not argue that the student who came 6th was twice as inferior as the person who came 3rd. The general point then is that the sets of numbers obtained from measurement procedures do not always have the characteristics inherent in the formal number system, so that certain arithmetic operations will lead to invalid descriptions of the real world.

This fact has led social scientists like Stevens[13] and Coombs[14] to classify the main types of scale which are produced by the operations used in measurement. Apart from the use of numbers simply to label objects (like members of a football team), the weakest *level of measurement* is the *ordinal scale* in which objects are ranked from 'least' to 'most' on some attribute—that is placed in order—but where the numbers do not convey the absolute amount of the attribute, or even how far apart the objects are with respect to the attribute. An example of an ordinal measure is socio-economic status or athletic ability as assessed by a person's rank position in a sports contest. With this level of measurement none of the fundamental operations of arithmetic—addition, subtraction, multiplication and division—may be meaningfully applied to the numbers obtained.

A somewhat stronger level of measurement is provided by the *interval scale* in which the numbers assigned to objects represent both their order on some attribute and the distance between them, but not their absolute position relative to some zero point. This applies, for example, to the measurement of temperature on a Centigrade scale or to the measurement of height if the unusual procedure were adopted of expressing each person's height relative to the shortest person in the group. With this scale addition and subtraction are permissible but not multiplication and division. Thus we can justifiably say that the difference in heat between $20°$ C and $15°$ C is the same as the difference between $15°$ C and $10°$ C, but we cannot say that $20°$ C is twice as hot as $10°$ C because the positioning of the zero point is quite arbitrary, and if it were moved the $2:1$ ratio would change.

The strongest level of measurement to which most scientists aspire, but which is rarely feasible in the social sciences, is that embodied in the *ratio scale*. Measurements at this level have all the properties inherent in our formal number system. That is objects may be placed in order, their distances on an attribute specified, and their position relative to the zero point also implied by the numbers produced in measurement. Examples of this scale are the measurement of height or weight; here we can meaningfully talk of differences in height and also specify ratios of height without producing empirically suspect statements. Thus in a ratio scale the empirical properties of an attribute are entirely *isomorphic* with the properties of the number system so that the number system becomes an accurate model of an aspect of the real world.

In practice most of the measures used in the social sciences—individual attributes such as aptitude or personality, and group measures such as cohesiveness, levels of prejudice or competitiveness—satisfy the criteria of an ordinal scale, and no more. However most of the traditional methods of statistical analysis require arithmetic operations which are only legitimate for higher levels of measurement. Thus correlational techniques, analysis of variance, and even the calculation of the arithmetic mean violate the properties of the ordinal measurements usually obtained by the researcher. Until comparatively recently the choice was between using these powerful techniques of analysis on data which did not strictly justify their use, or attempting to solve complex research problems with statistical tools that were legitimate but ineffective. The dilemma is gradually being resolved through the development of *non-parametric* statistical techniques which provide powerful analogues to conventional statistical tests but without assuming anything more than ordinal levels of measurement.[15] At the same time researchers are beginning to calculate the errors and distortions involved in using techniques which assume interval scales on measures which only approximate to this level of measurement. Generally speaking opinion seems to be moving towards the freer use of statistical techniques based on interval measurement except where this would involve a gross distortion of the empirical properties of the data.[16] It is still essential to select a measurement strategy which is consistent with the research design and proposed methods of analysis. In particular the researcher should avoid using measurements based on ranking (ordinal scale) if he wishes to employ a multi-factorial analysis of variance (see pp. 81–84) since this technique assumes interval measurement on a continuous, normally distributed variable.[17]

Fieldwork and correlational designs 3

In this chapter we shall deal with those designs in social research which, as a rule, provide us with descriptive material and correlational evidence, leading frequently to indirect and low-level tests of causal connections between social phenomena. Under this rubric we include sample surveys carried out in the field or applied to documentary material, fieldwork not based on statistical sampling procedures and including both interviewing and observational approaches, and the use of existing documentary material where no sampling is involved. All these approaches are non-experimental, although some sample survey designs may be described as quasi-experimental.

The experimental design is characterised by its ability effectively to control or to randomise all the extraneous variables (this is to be dealt with in detail in chapter 4). The drawback with experiments is that frequently they cannot combine this effectiveness of control with adequate representation of the universe to which inferences are made. The reverse is true of some designs used for descriptive or correlational studies. This is so in the case of sample surveys carried out in the field, where control populations are as a rule not available but where a high degree of representativeness may be achieved. Where field studies are carried out an additional advantage appears in that the research takes place in a natural setting. The latter is maximised where observational designs are used and is non-existent where a design is based on the use of desk evidence. Both the experiment and the sample survey fall, in this respect, somewhere between the two extremes. Whereas the laboratory experiment may simulate a natural setting but never quite attains this, the sample survey usually takes place in the natural setting in the field, on to which an artificial superstructure is imposed, i.e. formal interviews, set questionnaires, etc.

'Field study' is an umbrella term which covers three possible basic approaches: *(a)* the application of a statistical sampling procedure followed up by direct interviewing of varying degrees of formality or by the use of postal questionnaires; *(b)* participant observation, whether open or concealed; and *(c)* the interviewing of 'key contacts' or 'informants', usually without resorting to sampling methods. Which one of these approaches one should adopt depends principally on the type of information sought. Morris Zelditch uses for this purpose a threefold classification:[1] (i) *incidents* and *histories,* as for instance descriptions of events (rioting, a wedding, etc.) or of a sequence of events; (2) *distributions* and *frequencies,* as for instance the possession by members of a population of certain attributes (blue eyes); and (3) *generally known rules* and *statuses,* as for instance how political leaders are chosen or what status levels there are in a group. It should be fairly clear that statistical sampling procedures applied to vast populations are unnecessary and inefficient for obtaining information about certain rules in the political power game of a society. It is equally true that no amount of observation will ever provide us with any knowledge about, say, fertility trends in a country.

Consequently the research designer's first task is to decide which of the approaches are best suited for obtaining different types of information. Complex designs will be necessary when a study requires both hard statistical data, best obtainable by means of probability sampling or census-type enumerations, and the type of information which is best obtained through more flexible interviews (depth interviewing, focused interviewing) and observational techniques. The determining factors of design adopted include, besides the type of information sought, considerations of the cost involved, the situation in which the study would be undertaken, and so on. (Some further points on research strategy will be considered briefly in Chapter 5.) We shall now turn to the details concerning the main principles involved in different types of field study and correlational design.

SAMPLE SURVEYS

The basic premise in sampling a universe[2] is that the selection of a relatively small number of units on a scientifically arranged random basis will provide a sufficiently high degree of probability that this is a true reflection of the universe, that inferences may be made from the findings of the sample to the universe which is being scrutinised. In other words, 'random' or 'probability' sampling obtains what in common parlance is known as 'a cross-section of the population', a fact that enables the researcher to generalise within known limits of error from the sample to the population. The units one wishes to sample will vary; they may be individuals, households, schools, groups of people, or interactions between people. Sampling interactive as well as non-interactive units has become possible largely due to innovations in the collection of *sociometric-type* data, that is where the questions asked from the respondent refer explicitly to his relations to other specific individuals.[3] In this way families may be used as the units of enquiry and the relations within the family may be studied.

Using family units we could also discern the social relations within a community and examine the connections, say, between the social structure and the values held in the community. Thus, the question may be posed whether social ties in some groups are based largely on similarities in background and religion or on common leisure interests and other organisational activities.[4]

Even larger units of enquiry, such as organisations, may be used in order to characterise and analyse the organisation itself as well as the individual within it. The larger units, however, are still most frequently used only as stages leading to the final unit of enquiry, which is usually an individual respondent (this is explained below).

We shall now consider the main principles involved in the many different types of sample survey design and provide some examples showing the suitability of these designs in different situations and investigations. (A clear and more detailed exposition of these designs will be found in Moser and Kalton, *Survey Methods in Social Investigation*.[5])

There is only one sure way of reducing bias arising through sampling, Moser and Kalton say, and that is by using a random method. 'Randomness lies at the base of all sound sample designs; these designs differ chiefly in the refinements introduced to minimise sampling errors.'[6] As we shall see, however, some designs veer away from, or completely abandon, the principle of randomness. Even in designs where the basic principle of randomness is maintained modifications of the ideal model are made. This ideal model is simple random sampling, where every unit of the universe has an *equal chance* of being selected into the sample. Some modifications may partly contravene this rule in that they insure only that each unit in the universe has *some chance* of selection, but tend to reduce bias by refinements in the design of selection.

Let us look at some of these modifications. We shall divide them into two groups. In Group A we include those sampling designs which observe the basic idea of randomness and to which, as a result, it is possible to apply probability theory. The latter means that statistical figures obtained from such samples may be said to apply to the universe from which it has been drawn, with the qualifying statement that these figures are *probable* rather than *certain*, so far as the universe is concerned, since they are subject to some error due to the chances involved in sampling. In Group B we include those sampling designs which are not based on truly random selection and to which, therefore, probability theory does not apply. The critical factors which usually determine which design is adopted are: *(a)* the sampling frames available; *(b)* the speed with which the investigation has to be carried out; and *(c)* the relative cost of the design.

Group A

Stratified sampling. The magnitude of the uncertainty, mentioned above, regarding results emanating from sample data is determined primarily by the variability existing among units in a universe. It follows, therefore, that the less the variability the greater the certainty with which we can make inferences from the sample to the universe. The larger the sample size the lower the uncertainty, i.e. the error that may arise. We can usually identify certain groupings or strata in a universe. This means that there is greater homogeneity within each stratum than within the universe as a whole. Thus, leisure pursuits tend to vary less within age groups (old, middle-aged and young) than within a population covering all ages. Providing we know enough to identify which age groups are important we can select individuals for our sample within each group separately. This method is called 'stratified sampling' and leads to greater precision. The second source of error remains. That is, variations in the type of leisure activities, within say, the young age group, will still exist and by drawing separately the subsample of young people we still cannot be sure that we shall accurately reflect their leisure pursuits. Furthermore, only if the stratification factors are related to the topic of enquiry is anything to be gained from stratified sampling. Thus, stratification by hair-colour is irrelevant in a study of occupational distribution and, therefore, of no' avail when selecting the sample.

Multi-state sampling. Where the universe consists of a very large number of units spread over a wide area, and especially where there is no complete sampling frame easily available, one can resort to a design which entails a random selection of differently sized units at successive stages, leading to a sample of the final units of enquiry. An easy example of this would be the case of a survey of primary school children. A straightforward sample to be taken from the thousands of primary schools up and down the country would be too daunting to attempt, and it would result in an unnecessarily laborious task. Instead, one proceeds by taking a sample of regional government areas (Stage 1). Within the areas

34

chosen one selects a sample of education authorities (Stage 2). From the lists of primary schools in the latter sample one selects a sample of schools (Stage 3). Finally, the sample of schools provides the universe of schoolchildren from which the sample actually to be surveyed will be chosen (Stage 4).

This approach reduces time and cost in surveys without abandoning the principle of randomness throughout the stages involved. This example may also illustrate a design known as *cluster sampling*. We may decide not to proceed to Stage 4, but to include in the survey all the children in the schools selected at Stage 3. This means that although the unit of enquiry remains the same, i.e. the schoolchild, the sample taken is one of clusters of schoolchildren. Two points should be noted. Since human populations are not well mixed, that is groups of people with different characteristics, for example of age and social class, tend to concentrate in certain parts of a city, it tends to be more reliable to choose a large number of small clusters (streets or census enumeration districts), rather than a small number of large clusters (whole postal areas).[7] This raises the issue of what constitutes a cluster of units as against *the* unit of enquiry. The answer lies in identifying the most meaningful and useful unit of enquiry for the survey planned. Thus, in a survey of the administrative aspects of the provision of schooling, the local education authority may prove the most useful unit, in which case the cluster may be a whole region of a country. But in the case of equipment and educational methods used in schools, the school itself would be the most useful unit of enquiry and, therefore, the cluster would be the local education authority.[8]

Multi-phase or filter sampling. If we want to collect a limited amount of basic information from a large sample and to get more intensive data from a smaller subsample, we use a filtering process to obtain the latter. A specially designed question is introduced to identify members of the subsample, e.g. we include a question about identification with a religious denomination so that we may separate off a particular religious group. This technique is also particularly useful where the subsample represents a section of the universe with special characteristics, e.g. highly trained scientists, or in cases where the subsample would otherwise be difficult to locate, such as a recently settled immigrant group. Multi-phase sampling is also used simply to lighten the burden on respondents and investigators alike of a lengthy enquiry to the entire sample or universe. In the decennial census basic questions are asked from everyone but more details, for instance about educational attainments, are requested only from 10 per cent of the population.

Systematic sampling. This is a most frequently used method where a list, e.g. the Register of Electors, provides the sampling frame from which every *n*th name or address is systematically selected. The double proviso is that the start of the systematic selection is randomly determined and that the mode of listing of the units in the sampling frame has in no sense any relevance to the subject of the survey. Thus an alphabetical listing as a rule introduces an element of randomness in the frame itself, in that it is unlikely for it to be connected with, say, a study of political attitudes. So although strictly speaking this design departs marginally from the basic principle of random sampling it may be accepted as a fair approximation to it.

Group B

Quota or judgmental sampling : This is a method of sampling which is non-random in that the selection of the final unit of enquiry is left to the judgment of the interviewer. There is an attempt here to produce representativeness by means of 'quota controls', by stratifying the sample to be chosen in terms of certain basic population characteristics about which information is available from census and other well established sources. Thus, certain proportions of interviews will be allocated according to such proportions extant in the population of the country (i.e. the statistical universe), that is in terms of area, town size, age, sex, occupation, etc., as well as specific controls being applied according to the subject of the survey, e.g. control by educational attainments as, for instance, in a study which examines people's views regarding major changes in the educational field. There are two major problems in quota sampling. Where we multiply controls so as to increase representativeness, especially if these are applied not independently but in an interrelated fashion,[9] the task of the interviewer becomes almost unmanageable. Human judgment, and therefore the possibility of bias, still comes in where certain controls such as 'social class' are less easily ascertainable.[10] Quota sampling avoids sampling frames and preparatory work in the field, and is therefore cheaper and quicker so long as it is not weighed down by elaborate controls. It is useful for testing opinion quickly so as to avoid *memory errors* or *subject contamination,* e.g. in audience research and pre-election forecasts. Quota samples are, however, not true random samples.

Snowball sampling. This technique relies on the chain reaction built up from a few contacts which facilitates the interviewing of their friends, relations or colleagues, providing a system through which a special group, which is difficult to penetrate otherwise and for which no sampling frame exists, may be investigated. Good examples of such groups are deviants and some ethnic minorities. For building up the sample reliance is usually put on a number of key 'reference persons'. It is obvious that such interviews do not constitute random sampling and the technique must be regarded as highly individualistic. One element of bias accrues from the fact that the respondents may all come from a few closed circles. Another element of uncertainty is introduced by the fact that there appears to be no way in which the few initial contacts can be selected by a system which guarantees the avoidance of all bias.

Our specific concern, so far, has been to give an outline of the various methods available for selecting the units which go to make up a sample. Some designs combine two or three of these methods. We can combine multi-stage and multi-phase sampling. At the final stage we introduce a filter so as to begin phase two, closely scrutinising a special subsample. After choosing our units for the sample we still have to take the critical decisions whether to study one or several samples and what temporal sequences to adopt.

These decisions determine the extent to which quasi-experimental conditions may be achieved. The major alternative designs are set out in the chart below. These designs are then discussed in some detail.

Typological chart of survey designs

A	ONE-SHOT CASE STUDY	One sample is studied at one point of time. Aim: description; only rudimentary analysis usually involved.
B	ONE GROUP RECURRENT STUDY	Panel design, i.e. the same sample is studied several times. Aim: to discover change/trend in the group. Causal hypotheses may be formulated but not tested.
C	COMPARISON GROUPS EX POST FACTO STUDY	After the event designs: *type a :* cross-sectional. Aim: analysis of relationships between variables; *type b :* target/control groups. Aim: to discover effects of a test variable.
D	COMPARISON GROUPS – RECURRENT STUDY	Longitudinal designs with comparison groups. Aim: to test hypotheses re: change/trend. Several types: *type a :* cohort-sequential design; *type b :* time-sequential design; *type c :* cross-sequential design. See diagram below.

The one-shot survey *(A)* can describe a situation in static terms but cannot throw much light on whether it is due to a factor or factors, suggested by theory based on other data. A survey of a population may show that an immigrant group is not integrated into the larger society. Respondents may offer several reasons for this, e.g. that there is prejudice against immigrants, that immigrants are clannish due to their distinct religion, etc. The one-shot survey, design *A*, could not possibly show which one of these factors is the more potent. The recurrent study, design *B,* however, could indicate that the majority remains prejudiced against immigrants who have ceased to practise their religion, or alternatively that religious practices continue to prevent integration even when prejudices are drastically reduced. Clearly, such a study enables the investigator to formulate, say, the hypothesis that prejudice is the single most important factor in preventing integration. For testing such an hypothesis we would need, however, *comparison groups*. For instance it may be that the prejudice of the majority will prevent a coloured group from integrating but not a white minority. In other words, it may be that the truly crucial factor determining the integrative process in the long run is a lack of visibility and the concomitant ability of 'passing' for a member of the dominant society. Proof of this could only come from survey design D which involves a comparison of groups studied recurrently over a fairly long period of time.

As soon as we leave the 'one-shot' survey, which has only limited usefulness, we encounter problems as we apply the more complex designs. In the case of 'panel surveys' the problems of obtaining the initial sample, sample attrition and conditioning have to be faced. Volunteers to a panel would not meet the requirements of representativeness, whilst a representative sample willing to be interviewed or observed at intervals over a longer period of time is difficult to obtain. Over time our sample suffers attrition through death, illness, moving away, and change of mind regarding cooperation. Panel conditioning arises through an arousal of interest in the respondent and through his learning to play a special role, factors which destroy the representativeness of the sample, i.e. the sample becomes in a sense a special sub-group atypical of the universe studied.

The cross-sectional design (C, type a) involves picking different samples of respondents, all the samples together providing through comparison evidence of relationships between variables or evidence of causes of change. Panel conditioning does not operate since all the samples are studied only once and at the same time. A good example would be where different samples represent different age groups in the population. Supposing we investigate attitudes to political issues and find a close correlation between more advanced age and political conservatism. May we conclude that as we grow older we become more conservative? No, because the respondents in the different cohorts were born in different years and, therefore,

39

had different political experiences. We must not confound age differences with time of birth differences. We may be able to overcome this particular problem by adopting a longitudinal design (discussed below).

'After-the-event' designs of the target/control type $(C,$ type $b)$ are particularly suitable for testing the effectiveness of some newly introduced variable. Thus, if we select two comparable samples and test their attitudes to immigrants after showing one of the samples a race relations documentary film, we could draw certain conclusions regarding the effectiveness of particular educational instruments in shaping attitudes to immigrants. (This design is technically an *experiment,* see chapter 4.) It is important to note here that there are several levels of rigour of comparability of samples. At a lower level the target and control groups (samples) are *matched* in terms of frequency distributions for various characteristics. That is, the two groups have the same age and sex distributions, occupational distributions, etc. A more stringent method is *pairing,* i.e. precision matching. This means that, say, a mechanic, aged twenty, single, of a family of five, with formal education terminated at the age of fifteen, who is selected for the target sample would have his counterpart with exactly the same personal data in the control sample. The height of rigour is the allocation of these matched individuals to the target and control groups through *randomisation,* i.e. making sure that it is left to chance which matched units will fall into which groups. Rigorous matching for target/control designs becomes difficult when the representative samples become large.

Longitudinal studies *(D),* i.e. repeated measurements of the same samples over time, have been used to very good effect in developmental studies connected with biological, psychological and sociological research. The design is said to be able to show 'the nature of growth and trace patterns of change in the individual', and it is also asserted that it is the only method which can give 'a true picture of cause and effect relationships over time'.[11] As we have said, the cross-sectional design could produce a picture of development over time but its reliability is somewhat doubtful because of its composition of different cohorts. On the other hand retrospective studies, i.e. 'after-the-event' investigations would often be even worse. On this point Wall and Williams state: 'Where earlier status is variable—for example, height, weight, general ability, vocabulary—or where forms of behaviour are difficult to recall and describe accurately—for example, aggressiveness, shyness and withdrawal—retrospective information is of little or no value; and it is peculiarly liable to distortion in the light of subsequent knowledge.'[12]

But longitudinal designs also have their weaknesses. As with panel designs sample attrition may be a problem. After a longer period, therefore, comparability of the initial and final groups becomes somewhat shaky. However, at least one survey in Britain has lasted more than twenty years and maintained the interest and participation of 90 per cent of the original large representative sample of 5,000.[13] Again, as with panel studies, the sample may become conditioned and some disturbing variables may enter between recurrent measurements. The crucial fault in this design seems to be the possibility that if comparability is to be maintained, which is, after all, a prerequisite of longitudinal studies, new data, new hypotheses, new theories and methods that come to light from other research may be ignored. Most longitudinal designs do not encourage even the feedback of their own interim results and thus do not satisfy the consequent need for a re-evaluation of the study in progress.[14]

Cohorts			Age⟶	cross-sectional			
Date of birth							
1950	5	10	15	20	Longitudinal		
1955		5	10	15	20		
1960			5	10	15	20	
1965				5	10	15	20
	1955	1960	1965	1970	1975	1980	1985

Measurement intervals

Fig. 3.1   Cross-sectional and longitudinal sampling.

Figure 3.1 shows the two basically different designs: cross-sectional and longitudinal. In order to overcome the confounding of the various sources of change certain *sequential designs* may be suggested. The *cohort-sequential* design is one in which two cohort groups, that is two rows in the diagram, are studied simultaneously. In this way, changes due to age are separated from possible changes due to measurements taken at specific times for any one of the groups. The *time-sequential* design involves the study of two columns. This separates out the age differences from the effects of being born in one year rather than another. These designs are useful particularly in studies of child development. A design which combines both elements of the above, that is where at least two rows *and* two columns are included, is known as a *cross-sequential* design. The latter is particularly suitable for studying the effects of environment over time on adults.[15]

Before turning our attention to designs which do not involve sampling procedures, we should mention that in a given universe we may sample not only *spatial units* or *individual respondents* but also *events, time* during which certain events occur, and *documents*. In sampling events the greatest problem is definition. A broad definition would include certain social processes, like an inflationary spiral, which are complex and of long duration, and therefore, cannot be sampled. Other events, however, such as marriage ceremonies or football matches, are of relatively short duration and occur frequently. These are suitable for sampling. The investigator in planning his sampling of events must ensure: *(a)* that his universe includes only events that are strictly comparable; and *(b)* that the events are theoretically relevant to his investigation.

Time sampling techniques have been used particulary by child psychologists.[16] The universe could be the working day, say 7 a.m. to 7 p.m. The day is then divided into intervals of, say, five minutes. From the total of 144 time units a randomly selected sample of 25 per cent would provide thirty-six during which children's activities in a particular setting, such as a hospital, could be observed. Another example of time sampling is the study of the behaviour of car drivers on roads. This approach has the advantage of spreading observations or measurements randomly over the time span, and thus presumably attaining greater representativeness, without too much difficulty. Considered against the wider canvas of social research, time sampling sets greater problems especially where the design normally relies simply on space sampling. In connection with the latter certain assumptions may be questioned. For instance, does the time of the day when interviews are carried out matter; and if so should these not always be randomised? Or again, what is the effect of a particular season of the year on people's responses? And, of course, the majority of studies, particularly in sociology, are synchronic except for longitudinal designs where the specific objective of the investigations is change through time. Only where replications are made (see below) is the diachronic angle usually introduced; but more often than not the possibility of random selection of time is ignored in replication work. But since we know too little of how time variability may affect very many investigations in the social sciences, the time factor plays too small a part in sampling techniques.[17]

Document sampling is the simplest choice when the universe is clearly defined by the existence of a reliable sampling frame and when the documents are fully standardised. The best example is the population census a small fraction of whose forms is usually sampled in the first instance in order to release preliminary results quickly.[18] Similarly, the employment cards in a factory or personal data cards kept by an institution provide excellent opportunities for sampling. On the other hand most historical documents, e.g. autobiographies, diaries, letters, etc., are not suitable material for sampling, for two reasons. First, such material is of an individual nature and therefore the units sampled are not comparable. Second, as a rule such documents must usually be regarded as representing a self-selective sample with a particular bias (i.e. people have special reasons for producing such documents when not solicited, and special abilities to produce them). This sort of material is only useful where the procedure involves an examination of all existing documents leading to a careful content analysis[19] (see below).

DESIGNS WITHOUT STATISTICAL SAMPLING

Strictly speaking the term 'census' does not refer exclusively to complete enumerations but signifies more broadly the methods of obtaining basic demographic, economic and social data for a country. While much sampling work is now undertaken for various aspects of national censuses,[20] the latter still provide the best examples of the complete coverage of a universe. The principle of universality is appropriate to basic population data, for only by complete enumeration[21] can information contemporaneously be made available for all geographic areas, however small, and the basis for subsequent sampling work be established. This is why complete enumerations are undertaken usually at ten-yearly intervals. The problems of designing full censuses are complex. First, there is the weight of sheer organization and coordination, involving over 100,000 enumeration districts and nearly 97,000 enumerators. Enumeration districts must be numerous and small, usually comprising only some one hundred households, so as to enable the enumerators to control effectively and check carefully the assigned area in order to achieve full coverage.[22] Second, there is the need for accurate response which is not enhanced by additional questions. As Benjamin points out: 'Any progressive elaboration of the schedule is likely to reach a stage at which indifference, if not resentment, will introduce inaccuracy, and this may cause doubt to be cast on the validity of the whole enumeration.'[23] Third, the need for comparability between successive census data introduces a dilemma, since redefinitions of crucial terms in a census, e.g. 'dwelling', and 'household', 'occupation', and 'socio-economic groups', are necessary in the light of changing conditions.

Again, the crucial methodological aspect in designing complete coverage to produce enumerative and quantifiable data, if necessary, for smaller areas, lies in devising an approach which will yield essential basic information which has a high degree of validity and comparability. The investigator studying a factory or a village community has few internal organisational problems and once he has established rapport his informants cooperate. His main concern is to ask basic questions which through complete coverage will yield material against which the findings obtained through other techniques may be checked, and to obtain material that is comparable with other similar investigations. Anthropologists covering smaller areas, which can be regarded as intensive studies of small sample communities, have adopted a census-type approach, asking for instance for data about 'kinsmen' (e.g. names, clan affiliation, dates and number of marriages, details about children, etc.), and about other 'personal' facts (e.g. religious affiliation, occupation, labour history, crop sales, succession, etc.).[24]

The traditional anthropologist, however, is nearer his metier when he becomes a participant observer in a small primitive community. Full participation in alien cultures is not always possible; nor is it always successful where one wishes to participate in a subcultural group, e.g. where a middle-class researcher investigates a working-class area or takes up work in a factory. The observation may have to be from the sidelines or the researcher may even in some circumstances conceal his interests in observing people's behaviour. Whatever the types and nuances of the observations and whether the researcher is an anthropologist or a sociologist working in a contemporary society, the techniques of observation which include informal interviewing of 'key contacts' or of 'passing-by' informants, have certain characteristics which suggest a rough framework of design.

The characteristics depend on whether we use a structured or unstructured approach. Observational techniques, except those carried out by psychologists in experimental conditions (see chapter 4), are unstructured. The main characteristics are: *(a)* non-standardisation; *(b)* effective use of the relationship the researcher establishes with informants in the field for eliciting data.[25] These characteristics indicate the main practical requirements:

1. *The necessity for complete familiarisation with the field.* In an alien culture or in a subculture this means learning the language and the customs; in one's own culture as well as in an alien

45

culture familiarisation is to be gained also by acquiring all possible background information e.g. history, geographical layout of area, economic, social, political and religious set-up, etc.

2. *The necessity for winning the confidence of informants.* This need will determine which of the different 'observer roles' the invest-igator will assume—in an exclusive secretive sect where observers do not gain admittance he may have to conceal his true role; in a large open community he has the choice of playing his role in a concealed or open fashion; in a small closed community e.g. village or tribe, he has to reveal his role as scientific observer, but the extent to which he will be allowed to participate, or will wish to participate, in the life of the community will depend on the relationship between observer and observed.

3. *The task of ensuring accurate recording.* This is a serious problem since continuous and careful recording may be impossible or partly impeded; the whole essence of this technique is to concentrate on observing and communicating without interruptions, thus leaving the recording until after the observations. This may introduce errors and biases.

But this can be overcome by checking the reliability of data by repeated observations of a class of phenomena, either by the same observer or preferably by different observers. But is this feasible? On the one hand one may argue that the observer in the field can carry out observations of only *some* of the activities, responses, etc. of his subjects and that his observations are in fact only slices from a larger whole. Hence, although this does not amount to statistical sampling, it is sampling nonetheless, and therefore similar slices, responses, activities, etc. may be observed several times, making reliability tests possible. On the other hand one could stress that the essence of observations in the field is to comprehend the 'wholeness' of a situation over a longer period of time, e.g. the activities in their natural full setting, so that a repetition of 'whole' observations of such a nature is hardly feasible. Reliability testing would, therefore, not be possible. This view is reinforced by N. K. Denzin's definition of the essential features of participant observation: 'Participant observation is deliberately unstructured in its research design so as to maximise the discovery and verification of theoretical propositions. The attempt is to continually revise and test emergent hypotheses as the research is conducted.'[26] This implies that observation, measurement and analysis are intertwined so that they continually affect one another; hence the repetition of a similar process in the immediate research situation with the intent of reliability checking, is pertinent and viable only in the case of structured situations, but not in this case.

Statistical sampling also runs into difficulties where we are using basically non-standardised documentary evidence. Nevertheless, Johan Galtung maintains that statistical sampling procedure may be applied here too.[27] His examples come mainly from the mass media and he regards the universe as 'everything written about something', the boundaries of the universe to be drawn by four criteria: the place where the material was written, say the United Kingdom; the date when the written material appeared, e.g. 1 January 1972 to 31 December 1972; the form or medium of communication, e.g. a daily morning newspaper; and the topic involved, say Northern Ireland. Granted that the universe can in this way be delimited, it is very dubious if the unit subjected to investigation will be sufficiently standardised to allow sampling. For instance several variables make a unit such as 'the editorial' non-comparable. Thus the length of editorials vary; sometimes they pass judgment on past events and at other times they advise and predict, etc. Above all, some are definitely linked with a particular incident or a particular longer article, whilst others refer in a more general tone to the topic discussed.

On the other hand if the unit is some word, e.g. democracy, sampling it is of limited use, for what matters is the *context* in which the reference occurs. The problems apply to other documentary sources, e.g. parliamentary speeches, private diary material, etc. which are not standardised. While it is inadvisable to sample such material, we can use content analysis, either of the type which results in quantification or of the interpretative variety which produces qualitative information. The former type of content analysis is defined as 'a research technique for the objective, systematic and quantitative description of the manifest content of communication'.[28] Its basic advantage over direct questioning is that it is *non-reactive,* that is it would be unusual to find masking and sensitivity of the sort where the producer of the data knows he is being studied by a social scientist.[29] Another advantage is that we can cover a long period of time. The basic distinction is between the approach which aims at analysing the *manifest* (see definition above) pattern of attitudes or descriptions of behaviour in the documentary evidence examined, and the approach which aims at discovering the *latent* meanings of such behaviour or of attitudes communicated. The *manifest* patterns will normally lead to quantitative results. For instance, one can measure the *length* of articles devoted to a certain topic in newspapers, the *number* of times certain words occur in certain contexts, the *sequence* in which topics are dealt with, and so on. Examination of the *latent* meanings of documents, normally produces qualitative material which gives us a deep and full understanding of certain attitudes expressed, or of the functioning of whole organisations. In studying organised entities by the aid of this method Bryan Wilson points out: 'Documents must be critically assessed; compared; related to the documentary and the action context of the occasion of their creation; examined for intrinsic inconsistencies, compromise and defense statements; and understood in terms of the position of those responsible for them.'[30]

Content analysis, as most other techniques, cannot stand alone. It can produce very useful material, but the value of such material is usually augmented by data obtained through other techniques.

DESIGN OF FIELD INSTRUMENTS

Where direct questioning is necessary in field work three basic instruments may be used: *the questionnaire, the interview schedule* and *the interview guide.* Goode and Hatt define these as follows:

Questionnaire refers to a device for securing answers to questions by using a form which the respondent fills in himself.

Schedule is the name usually applied to a set of questions which are asked and filled in by the interviewer in a face-to-face situation with another person.

An interview guide is a list of points or topics which an interviewer must cover during the interview.[31]

We can of course combine certain aspects of these types of instrument, as in the case where an interviewer delivers a questionnaire, obtains the respondent's cooperation, but does not actually interview him, leaving him to fill in the questionnaire. Again, as we shall see below, an interview guide can include some more formalised questions. The advisability of various combinations depends on the research conditions or requirements where one or the other type of instrument or combination would have the greatest payoff. In this section our interest centres on the main principles and problems appertaining to these instrument types.

Whilst methodologists recognise more than three types of instrument along the continuum of rigid to flexible questioning, the above basic types exemplify, through the postal questionnaire and the interview schedule, instruments that are highly structured and normally completely rigid. The interview guide is, on the other hand, an example of a more flexible instrument.[32] The questionnaire and the schedule, therefore, have many features in common. We shall discuss these common features and also mention a few of the differences between the two instruments.

The highly structured and completely standardised instrument is designed to be a uniform stimulus. Variations which appear in responses can be attributed only to real differences in response and not to variation in the way the instrument works. There are several grounds for doubt as to whether such an aim can be achieved. The interview situation is a social encounter between two unique individuals. Thus we have a whole array of different interview situations according to the different relationship or 'rapport' struck up between interviewer and respondent. Furthermore, *subliminal cues* are at work on both sides, that is cues recognised only subconsciously but nonetheless capable of affecting the actual response given as well as the interpretation by the interviewer of the meanings of responses. Thus the slightest differences in gesture or tone of voice on both sides could distort the material gathered, whether factual or attitudinal. In the postal questionnaire the respondent may be influenced by others, who are irrelevant to the research; the respondent reading the whole questionnaire may distort his responses to make them appear logical and consistent. So we cannot really attain the standardisation of the stimulus, by using questions embedded in the highly structured types of instrument. To be more precise, the standardisation of the tool, i.e. the questionnaire or the schedule, is destroyed in the process of its application.

Another set of criticisms of these instruments is that they are culture-ridden and class-ridden. There are many subcultural variations in the meaning of certain words in a language, so that we cannot assume that all respondents are presented with the same stimuli eliciting the same range of meanings. Again, better educated people are more used to filling in questionnaires and being interviewed. And interviewers tend to be middle class, and so get different results from respondents from their own class or some other social class.

Finally, the problems of reliability and validity are said to loom large because of such factors as prestige, bias, or social desirability awareness, e.g. respondents exaggerate the time they spend on reading and understate the amount of alcohol they consume, and they often tend to express opinions which they believe to be socially acceptable rather than because of their own convictions.

The designer of these research tools has to take the criticism seriously. He can try to obviate the problems by taking the following steps. First, structuring and rigidity must be effective, not just nominal: in no circumstances may the wording be changed from one interview to another—questions, whether in the questionnaire or the interview schedule, are to be identical. The context of questions must also be identical, since this may influence their meaning and so must be the sequence of the questions. There are certain generally accepted ways of ordering questions: more interesting questions are put first, whilst highly emotional and embarrassing or threatening questions come in at the end.

Standardisation by means of closed questions further ensures that variability in responses is not due to faulty application of the instrument in the field. The built-in multiple-choice answers are often presented in a randomised pattern so as to avoid ordinal biases, i.e. the tendency for respondents to choose the average, or near the middle of a series. (On details of questionnaire design see Oppenheim's *Questionnaire Design and Attitude Measurement*.[33])

Second, the researcher must ensure that interviewers are fully briefed and trained. The inexperienced interviewer *improves* as he goes along; after some interviewing he puts his questions to the respondents more clearly, he attains better 'rapport', and so on. As a result the principle of *invariance* is destroyed. Certain standards required for the interview situation must be attained by the interviewers *before* the survey is launched. A more thorough training with the aim of attaining a uniform field application of questionnaire or schedule, attempting to eliminate any possible change in the interview situation or differences in wording and emphasis, could substantially reduce variability due to unique 'social interaction' influences. The use of tape-recorded questions by the interviewer could further ensure a higher degree of uniformity. Tape-recording the answers and recording them manually at the same time could provide further checks on the true meanings of responses. The last point leads more generally to the question of how to ensure reliability and validity. The former refers to consistency in responses, whilst the latter concerns the question whether items measure or evaluate what they are supposed to measure or evaluate. Reliability of factual questions may be ensured by means of *internal checks,* for example a man who claims to have fought in a certain war must be in a certain age group. In the case of attitudinal questions greater reliability will be achieved by applying multiple sets of opinion items, for instance through scaling devices, in order to elicit *underlying* attitudes. Validity, on the other hand, could be checked upon by alternative sources of information on the same topic, as in the case where factual data obtained in a survey is checked against relevant census data.

Third, the problem of cultural and social class influences must be tackled. The basic aim in questionnaires or schedules must be to construct them on a 'culture fair' principle. Only simple words, familiar to all social classes, should be used. Some words are loaded with particular meanings to different classes and subcultures—these must be avoided. Good examples of such words are: bosses, strike-breakers, reactionary, socialist. Similarly, certain phrases such as 'racial integration' produce leading questions,[34] again with different meanings attached to them by various clusters of the population, and therefore, they must be avoided. Oppenheim points out that split-ballot trials usually show considerable differences in the distribution of answers when loaded wording is used. Thus, respondents asked in a survey to say whether they were 'upper', 'middle' or 'lower' class answered 'middle' more often than those asked if they were 'upper', 'middle' or 'working' class.[35] In the interviewer-respondent interaction class bias or culture bias can be avoided on the one hand by using a mixed group of interviewers, that is of both sexes, of varied age-groups, and of all social classes and subcultures, for interviewing a heterogeneous population. On the other hand, with special populations such as ethnic minorities or religious groups, the interviewers have to be members of the groups studied, for there is evidence suggesting that a high degree of reliability could not otherwise be achieved.[36]

Unfortunately, the structured questionnaire and schedule cannot be made into faultless instruments, although more methodological research may help. But careful design can eliminate many of the faults. Most of the steps have the tendency, though, to make these instruments rigid. For this reason they are, on their own, most useful in investigations which seek fairly straightforward quantifiable information. Where we want more qualitative information the *interview guide* must be resorted to, for its greater flexibility makes it more suited for eliciting such material and for probing more complex aspects of social relationships. In many surveys the schedule combines pre-coded questions, often presented on cards rather than asked verbally, with open-ended questions and probings; the former provide the factual information, the latter the deeper attitudinal stuff and the replies to the 'why' and 'in what way' probings. A typical section of a schedule with such a combination is shown below.

Questions   *Codes*

7a. Do you identify yourself with any religious group? Yes......... Y
                                                        No......... X
                                                   Not Sure......... O

         (If Y coded ask 7b)

7b. Are you officially on the membership roll or otherwise have you done what is required (e.g. vows, confessions, etc.) to be accepted as a full member of any religious group?
                                                        Yes......... Y
                                                         No......... X

         (If Y coded ask 7c)

7c. What is the name of the religious group of which you are a member? ....

         (Ask all)

7d. I would like to ask you about your childhood awareness of belonging to a religious group. Which of these statements describe your awareness most accurately?

                          SHOW CARD

         It was a very important part of my childhood............ Y
         I was aware of it, but it was not of great importance...... X
         I was aware of it, but it was unimportant.................. O
         I was not aware of it.. I
         Don't know... 2

         (If Y coded ask 7e)

7e. In what way was it very important?.....................................
     ....

Now let us return to the interview guide. This is the tool used in connection with the *focused interview*. The interviewer relies mainly on a small number of open-ended questions around several major topics relevant to an enquiry. The communication between interviewer and respondent is highly flexible: the interviewer probes with more questions and changes the emphasis needed, and the respondent may add freely to the original information sought or change the sequence of topics or the emphasis he wishes to give to different topics. Although the focused interview is characterized by limited direction and a flexible structure, different levels of structuring may be built into the interview guide, as we shall see below. First, however, we look in some detail at the special implications of the focused interview for the research designer, as set out by R. K. Merton and his associates.[37]

The distinguishing characteristics of this technique are:

(a) the respondents are known to have been involved in a *particular situation,* e.g. they have seen a film or read a pamphlet;

(b) through a content analysis of the situation the social scientist sets up *hypotheses* regarding the consequences of the situation;

(c) from this the interview guide is developed setting up the *major topics* to be gone into;

(d) with the help of the interview guide the interviewer then focuses on the experiences of the persons exposed to the pre-analysed situation in order to ascertain *their definitions of the situation;*

(e) the responses obtained help to test the original hypotheses and since these usually include *unanticipated responses* they give rise to fresh hypotheses for further systematic examination.

There are four main criteria for achieving effective focused interviews.

1. The interview should enable respondents to maximise the reported *range* of evocative elements and patterns in the stimulus situation, as well as the range of responses.

2. The interview should elicit highly *specific* reports.

3. The interviewer should help respondents to describe in *depth* the meanings of the situation and the degree of their involvement in it.

4. The interview should bring out the *personal context* for respondents which endow the situation with distinctive meanings to them.

The actual operationalising of the focused interview can be exemplified by looking at the different levels of structuring that may be built into the questions.

1. *Unstructured question* (stimulus and response free), e.g. 'What impresses you most in this film?' or 'What stood out specially in this conference?'. This type of question gives an entirely free hand to the respondent and elicits varied types of responses.

2. *Semistructured question, type A* (response structured, stimulus free), e.g. 'What did you learn from this pamphlet which you hadn't known before?'; and *type B* (stimulus structured, response free), e.g. 'How did you feel about the part describing Joe's discharge from the army as psychoneurotic?' In the above guidance is obviously increased, but the informant still retains considerable freedom of reply.

3. *Structured question* (stimulus and response structured), e.g. 'Judging from the film, do you think that the German fighting equipment was better, as good as, or worse than the equipment used by the Allies?' Here complete control is assumed by the interviewer; not only is the item for comment singled out, but the possible responses are also given. Where structuring of this nature is introduced the focused interview merges into the formalised and rigid type of interview and loses its true characteristic.[38]

Merton, *et al.,* point to the best course of action when they say:

Although the fully unstructured question is especially appropriate in the opening stages of the focused interview, where its productivity is at a peak, it is profitably used throughout the interview. In some instances it may be necessary for the interviewer to assume more control at later stages of the interview, if the criteria of specificity, range, depth and personal context are to be satisfied. But even in such cases . . . moderate rather than full direction is fruitful; questions should be partially rather than fully structured.[39]

Using the kind of design proposed by Merton, especially the idea of equipping oneself with a prior analysis of the situation, puts the interviewer in an advantageous position. He can distinguish the objective facts from the subjective definitions given to these by the respondent. He is thus alerted to the patterns of selective response and is able to recognise symbolic or functional silences, distortions, avoidances or blockings. Consequently, the interviewer is well prepared to explore the implications of selective responses and is able to detect private logics, symbolisms, and tensions. In short, he can gauge *the importance of what is not being said,* as well as of what is being said. Above all, the interviewer, through prior or situational analysis, can elicit what the focused interview is really after, 'not whether an experience is "stimulating" or "unpleasant" but rather more precisely what "unpleasant" denotes in this context, which concrete feelings were called into play, which personal associations came to mind'.[40] In asking for a great deal of detail by means of a flexible instrument allowing continuous probings, and using the interview guide simply to keep on the basic research tracks, it may be argued that the respondent is less likely, either intentionally or unwittingly, to conceal his true reactions to a situation. On the other hand these advantages accrue only when the technique is used by highly experienced and skilful researchers. For there are many pitfalls by which the less experienced interviewer-researcher could be affected, so that the results would become invalidated. A combination of detachment and close interest is not easy to achieve. In protracted interviews, as focused interviews are bound to be, the interviewer may be tempted to voice his own opinion, to correct mistaken notions put forward by the respondent, to become educative in order to be able to discuss topics on his interview guide, or to show disappointment when information he is supplied with does not help him to test his hypothesis. Such temptations or lapses could easily convert the interview situation into a debating society or classroom situation. As a result the respondent is likely to be inhibited and to produce defensive remarks or spurious reports. The whole purpose of the focused interview could thus be destroyed.[41]

To sum up, let us note that the design of field instruments is intended to do two things: to translate the objectives of the research into an appropriate set of questions; and to maximise the potential value of the responses. Success in the selection of questions depends on the careful formulation of hypotheses or descriptive aims, and the rigorous analysis of which questions are logically relevant to those aims. Having chosen the right set of topics for the questions, the usefulness of the responses will depend on the skill with which the phrasing and presentation of questions are matched with the language and experience of the respondents, and finally on the interpretative abilities of the researcher.

PERPARING THE FIELD STUDY

In operationalising a field survey the first step is to produce, on the basis of the hypothesis, a fairly large number of mock tables and blank cross-tabulations; i.e. the stubs and captions without the data. If, for example, it is being hypothesised that there is a correlation between religious affiliation and type of occupation in a particular section of the community, a table like the one below will ultimately be required.

Religious affiliation	*Occupational distribution*			
	NON-MANUAL		MANUAL	
	Professional	*Managerial & white collar*	*Skilled*	*Semiskilled & unskilled*
Religion A				
Religion B				
Religion C				
Religion D				

This specimen cross-tabulation suggests to the researcher: *(a)* the kind of questions and categories that will have to be included in the interview schedule; *(b)* the minimum size of the sample.

57

Since there are sixteen cells in the data matrix a sample of, say, eighty respondents could hardly ensure that some cells would not have zero entries; and with small numbers of cases in each cell meaningful percentage comparisons and useful statistical tests of significance could not accrue; the minimum effective sample size, therefore, is much more likely to be 150 to 200 which would mean an average of about ten respondents per cell. Even then the sample size may have to be increased if there is a high degree of variability in the universe or if the researcher is aiming at statistical precision.[42]

It will also be necessary to increase the number of cells in the matrix if we wish to test for the possible spuriousness of the correlation, that is the possibility that religion and occupation are both influenced by a third variable such as ethnicity. If we wish to carry out such control testing for only three additional variables, say, ethnicity split into three categories (English, Irish, Indian), age split into two categories (below 30 and 30 or over) and type of area also split into two categories (urban and rural), the number of cells will increase from 16 to 192 necessitating a sample size of around 2000. In other words, as the number of cross-tabulations increases the required sample size will increase in a multiplicate fashion. The number and type of cross-tabulations will, of course, also influence the costing and organisation of the fieldwork and finally the technique of data analysis, a computer being highly desirable for the analysis of tabulations involving more than three or four variables.

Having specified the relationships of interest by means of mock tables, and after deciding on sample size, the researcher will then have to choose a sampling plan and design his measuring instruments. These two major steps have already been discussed in some detail and we shall now turn to the final stage of preparation, namely the performance of 'pre-tests' and 'pilot studies'. Pre-tests are fairly informal trial runs, such as doing a few test interviews or handing out a few questionnaires. This gives us the first indication of their effectiveness in the field and may suggest modifications to the form of questions so as to make them meaningful to respondents. The pre-tests will also show whether people are at all likely to cooperate. The pilot study on the other hand is 'a small-scale replica of the main survey'. It will highlight a number of points:

(a) the adequacy of the sampling frame;

(b) the variability of the population, pointing, therefore, to the most efficient sample design and the size of the sample necessary, i.e. the less variability with regard to the subject investigated the smaller the sample size required and vice versa;

(c) the non-response rate, which again will help in deciding on initial size of sample, i.e. in order to produce the required effective sample size;

(d) the suitability of the data collection technique, pointing to possible alternatives other than that tried in the pilot study;

(e) the adequacy of the questionnaire, particularly whether the questions provide the necessary indicators to identify and measure the variables under scrutiny and whether this is done in an unambiguous and meaningful way.

The pilot study will also throw light on the efficiency of the instructions and briefing of interviewers, help in deciding on how to pre-code certain questions, and tell us the probable cost and duration of the main survey, as well as indicate the overall efficiency of the researcher or team engaged in the study.[43] Overall, the pilot study should finally confirm or modify the design proposed, or possibly suggest an alternative to it before the researcher actually commits himself to the field work.

DESIGN AND COMPARABILITY

Comparability in the enormous number of social research projects now taking place is desirable for two main reasons: First, advance in the social sciences can only come about if research results are additive, a goal to be attained by standardisation of concepts and empirical measures. Second, the establishment of sound theories must depend on frequent replications and follow-up studies, the former to add support and the latter to monitor changes and developments.

Where the researcher is working within a narrow field, at a particular point in time, he may be only vaguely aware of the need for such comparability. In the context of comparative research, however, where the design may cover several cultures, societies or nation states, the need to achieve comparability and the problems involved are much more in evidence. There is no general agreement, for example, on the boundaries of comparability in cross-cultural and other comparative research. Some more cautious social scientists restrict their comparisons to 'sets of structurally similar cultures, societies, polities, etc.' e.g. feudal societies or advanced Western nations; other, more ambitious, comparativists 'seek to establish bases for comparisons across all known units, whether elementary cultures, transitional societies or complex empires and nation states'[44] in the hope of developing a universal social science. When designing diachronic comparative studies, e.g. the emergence and decline of bureaucratic empires over a long period of history, the problem of comparability is particularly acute. Since the only available evidence consists of secondary material which is bound to be uneven, the researcher is forced to use very broad categories for analysis which lack the sensitivity needed for relationships to emerge.

The problems are less daunting, but still very complex, where synchronically designed field studies across several sites are envisaged. It is not simply a question of ensuring, for instance, that a comparable sample survey is used within each national population. As the contributions of Lazarsfeld and Rokkan[45] indicate there are decisions to be made about the level of analysis at which comparisons are to take place. Rokkan points out that one may operate at 'the level of the elementary micro-units, e.g. the individual, the household, etc., and test propositions about the sources of variations at that level or at the higher level of contextuality', e.g. occupational groups, social class or large community; or again one might decide to analyse behaviour 'at the macro-level of the total nation and test out propositions on the sources of aggregate, structural or global variations'.[46] In the former case the accent is on the smaller units and the comparisons over national or cultural boundaries serve essentially as replication of micro-studies.[47] In the latter the units are global, i.e. entire societies, and the crossing of boundaries constitutes a macro-comparative study.[48]

As a rule the macro-comparative study is best suited to the development of grand theories, with universal bases, especially with regard to structural aspects of society. The micro-replication study, on the other hand, is particularly useful for extending the support for middle-range theories. There are, in addition, other aspects of a study (apart from national setting) which can be varied so as to produce useful replications of research. Galtung[49] specifies several of these, including replication with different levels of the original variable, and with different forms of the measuring instruments.

Cross-national studies and replications can only succeed if social scientists are agreed on the definitions of their concepts and if a move is made towards the standardisation of the main variables used in social research. This is a grassroots problem which has, in recent years, been looked into by sociologists in Britain concerned with survey work.[50] The view held is that 'some understanding in the national context is necessary before international comparability can be meaningfully approached'.[51] To achieve such a modicum of understanding the sights have been set fairly low: *(a)* the categories to be used in survey work were to be standardised in such a way that collapsibility would be ensured, allowing the researcher to design for his own specific needs but at the same time to present his material in a manner which makes it comparable with material on the same topic in other studies; *(b)* only 'key variables' or 'face-sheet variables' were in the first instance to be dealt with. Those that have already been studied and reported on include education, family and household, income, occupation, religion, housing and locality. Papers in preparation deal with age, sex and related topics, politics, race, stratification and membership of voluntary associations.[52]

Two examples may be mentioned briefly to illustrate the kind of recommendations put forward in order to achieve some of the aims mentioned above. For the variable 'occupation' it is stressed that the subject's present occupation should be recorded with length of time in the job and whether it is permanent employment. One should concentrate on the subject's main occupation, but if possible and relevant one should also collect a job history. Researchers are alerted to the fact that the classification 'retired' is inadequate, so that some data about previous occupations should be sought. A careful distinction between full-time and part-time working should be made; similarly between long-term and short-term unemployment. It is also noted that taking down merely the present occupation of the respondent is often insufficient for sociological research; the occupations of the other members of his domestic group should, therefore also be collected.[53] The recommendations on 'occupation' show a great deal of flexiblity and prove that the work of standardisation is not likely to put serious constraints on the researcher. For the variable 'religion' one of the suggestions made is that the large number of categories, of the type used by Gallup Poll enquiries for eliciting information about attendance at religious services, can be usefully condensed for many purposes into three broad categories. Those attending once a week and once a month are grouped together into a *regularly* category; those attending 'now and again' and on important 'holy days' go into the *occasionally* category; whilst those who normally do not attend except on family occasions such as weddings are classed together with those who listen to radio/TV services only or never attend, into a *do not attend* category. The use of *condensed categories* illustrates how easily collapsibility may be achieved and that the element of stadardisation enhances the comparability of the results of many studies whilst it still allows data to be presented in a detailed as well as a condensed form.[54]

More generally it has been recognized that to include a fairly large number of 'key variables', with certain ideally desirable categories, could overload many a survey schedule and would not be feasible for certain smaller-scale studies. Similarly, inadequate coverage of a long list of items without the detailed recording suggested is not advocated. Elizabeth Gittus expresses the hope, therefore, 'that investigators, with both the resources to extend their work beyond their immediate needs and the concern that their studies should be fed into a cumulating body of knowledge, will give some attention to the framework'[55] which attempts to achieve comparability by the standardization of 'key variables' in survey research.

CORRELATIONAL RESULTS

In this chapter we have discussed the kinds of research design through which it is possible to produce descriptive results and correlational evidence. Since none of the designs discussed is truly experimental, no direct evidence of causation can be said to emanate from such research. The kind of evidence we can obtain is that which shows that there exists a measure of association between two or more variables, i.e. that they tend to fluctuate together. But while an association is a necessary condition of causation it is not a sufficient condition, so that while a correlation might suggest the existence of a causal relationship, it does not provide by itself a basis for inferring causation.

It is, however, possible to move in the direction of causal inference by adopting a quasi-experimental design in which samples are matched for a number of extraneous variables, hence increasing the likelyhood that an observed correlation reflects causation. Since the independent variable cannot be manipulated however, and is merely allowed to vary naturally, such designs are not truly experimental (see pp. 40 and 64) There are other, more advanced, techniques for using correlational studies to support causal hypotheses and these are referred to in chapter 5.

Experimental methods

In the last chapter we discussed a whole range of techniques which were broadly classified as 'correlational' because they looked at the interrelationships between naturally occurring events. A lot can be learned by analysing the covariation between such events, and indeed this is often the only feasible method for studying social phenomena, but the approach suffers from one particular limitation; however sophisticated a correlational design may be, it is difficult to establish *causal* connections between variables with any degree of confidence. We may show for example, that among a group of schoolchildren of mixed ages weight and spelling ability are highly correlated with each other. But this does not imply that a child's performance in a spelling test is in any sense *caused* by his weight. It is much more likely that both these variables are influenced by a common third variable, age. So it is with all forms of correlated research. We can never exclude the possibility that an unmeasured variable is mediating the relationship between the two variables we observe. Hence the *causal* connection between smoking and lung cancer took many years to establish because the evidence was largely correlational and left open the possibility that there were common underlying factors, like eating habits or anxiety, which were mediating the observed relationship between smoking and cancer.

The great advantage of experimental methods is that they do not rely on the observation of naturally occurring relationships between variables. In experimental work the researcher actually manipulates one variable (the independent variable), holds all other variables constant, and then observes the effect of this manipulation on the behaviour of interest (the dependent variable). If a relationship emerges under these conditions one can be relatively certain that the independent variable is having a direct effect on the dependent variable. Hence the ideal test of the 'smoking—lung cancer' hypothesis would be an experiment in which one group of subjects were made to smoke, say, twenty cigarettes a day for ten years, and a second group of subjects, matched in all respects to the first, were prohibited from smoking. If the first group subsequently developed significantly more cases of lung cancer one could conclude with reasonable confidence that smoking (the independent variable) has a direct effect on the incidence of lung cancer (the dependent variable).

This example clearly demonstrates the power of experimental techniques over correlational studies. By exercising direct *control* over the relevant independent variables hypotheses can be tested more rigorously and *cause and effect* statements can be made with greater confidence. At the same time it is clear that experimental methods have only limited applications in social research either because they would involve too great a restriction on human rights, as in the hypothetical smoking experiment, or because the variables of interest are simply not amenable to direct manipulation. Many important variables in social research, for example age, sex, social class, personality, income, occupation and so on, come into this non-experimental category and under these conditions correlational methods must be adopted.

It is perhaps worth mentioning that many research designs are sometimes loosely referred to as experimental when, in fact, they are not. An example from psychology should make this point clear. Bruner and Goodman[1] were interested in the effect of wealth on children's judgment of the size of coins. They compared the performance of two groups of subjects, a rich group and a poor group, on size estimation and showed that the poor children did in fact overestimate coin size to a greater extent than rich children. At first sight this may appear to be an *experiment* in which the variable wealth is being manipulated and the resulting changes in size judgments observed. But the researchers did not actually manipulate wealth in the sense that one might manipulate a subject's hunger or smoking rate. Instead they simply *selected* subjects to fit their two categories of rich and poor. In other words they used natural variation of the independent variable (wealth) and examined its relationship to the dependent variable (size judgment). This is essentially a correlational design, and in this case it is easy to imagine a third variable—experience of handling coins—which might account for the apparent influence of wealth on judgments of coin size.

In order to convert this study into a true experiment one would have to find some way of actually manipulating wealth, which on the face of it seems hardly feasible. Nevertheless, some investigators have made an ingenious attempt to do this by using hypnotic suggestion to assign subjects to different—albeit artificial—states of wealth (Ashley, Harper and Runyon[2]). Under these somewhat unusual experimental conditions the 'poor' subjects still produce greater overestimation of coin size than the 'rich' ones which might be taken to support a causal link between the two variables.

Despite their widespread use, experimental methods frequently come under attack from many different quarters. It is sometimes suggested that human beings do not behave naturally under experimental conditions and that the results of such researches are therefore of very limited application. There is some truth in this argument, which incidentally applies equally to the use of questionnaire and survey designs. But it is possible to guard against artificial or unnatural behaviour in an experiment either by measuring the subject's behaviour without his knowledge (e.g. by using naturally available data from census results or voting statistics for groups exposed to different experimental treatments), or by concealing the presence of the experiment (e.g. by varying experimental treatments, say, alternative teaching methods, without informing the subjects of the variations until after the experiment).[3] There are yet other conditions in which it would seem unlikely that participation in an experiment would change the true relationship between dependent and independent variables. Hence

Lythgoe's observation of the relationship between stimulus brightness and visual acuity is unlikely to have been affected by his subjects' awareness of the experimental situation. Nevertheless it is still important to consider the possibility of unnatural behaviour when interpreting experimental findings in social research.

A second, somewhat different criticism is that experiments do not capture the essential features of real-life situations but merely isolate one or two variables from the mass of interacting factors present in reality. This statement is, of course, true, but it should not be thought of as a criticism of experimental methods so much as a misunderstanding of their purpose. The scientist is not interested in simply describing complex phenomena, but in understanding the causal events that lead up to them. To do this he must begin by analysing the interconnections between a few variables in carefully controlled 'pure' conditions. Once the properties of the main 'components' have been studied in isolation, it is possible to go on to examine their interactions with each other and ultimately to offer an explanation of the real-life phenomenon together with a basis for its prediction and control. But we could not expect to achieve such understanding simply by studying the uncontrolled changes in all the variables operating together in reality. At the very least such an approach must be combined, wherever possible, with an experimental analysis of the effects of all relevant variables, and interactions between variables, on the behaviour under study.

THE USE OF EXPERIMENTATION IN SOCIAL RESEARCH

To what extent are experimental methods useful to the social scientist? We have already shown that many important social variables cannot be manipulated experimentally, and, where they can, the use of experimental control would sometimes prove socially unacceptable. Nevertheless there remain a number of fields in which a rigorous experimental approach can be used to great advantage. Perhaps the most notable contribution to date has come from social psychologists interested in the determinants of small group behaviour. Much ingenuity has been shown in bringing such factors as stress, communication patterns, style of leadership, cohesiveness and so forth under direct experimental control, thereby revealing how these factors influence various aspects of group performance and efficiency. For example Harold Leavitt[4] performed a classic experiment on the effect of different communication networks on group behaviour. By varying the pattern of cummunication links between group members in different conditions Leavitt was able to demonstrate the effect of communication pattern on such variables as group efficiency, group satisfaction, and the emergence of group leaders.

Psychologists interested in various aspects of individual behaviour such as the acquisition on skills, or the detection of visual stimuli, also make regular use of experimental methods. This is hardly surprising as the important determinants of such behaviour are factors like length of training, stimulus brightness or stimulus duration which are readily brought under precise experimental control.

In contrast to the frequent use of experiments by psychologists it is sometimes argued that sociology is destined to remain a non-experimental science, depending, somewhat like astronomy, on the observation of naturally occurring events. Hence McGuigan argues as follows:

> In some sciences, sociology, for example, there is little hope that anything but non-experimental methods can be generally used. This is primarily because sociology is largely concerned with the effect of prevailing culture and social institutions on behaviour, and it is difficult to manipulate these two factors as independent variables in an experiment.[5]

But this view is unnecessarily pessimistic and hardly compatible with the increasing number of experimental field studies reported by sociologists, demographers, educational researchers, industrial sociologists and others. The work of Morse[6] is typical of this type of experimental field study. In this research the aim was to determine whether various organisational structures (democratic versus autocratic supervision) had significantly different effects on productivity. The experimenters actually manipulated the type of supervision adopted by two matched groups of organisations, and were able to show that the group receiving democratic control were more productive than the group of organisations subjected to autocratic control. Many similar sociological experiments are listed by Ross and Smith[7] and by French.[8]

EXPERIMENTAL CONTROL

We have already said that the power of an experimental design resides in its ability to keep all independent variables constant except the one *that is being investigated. The term *control* is thus used in the double sense of (1) holding most variables constant (we shall call these the extraneous variables), while (2) manipulating that variable whose effects are of interest to the researcher (we shall henceforth reserve the term independent variable for this). It is by the proper use of this dual control that the experimenter is able to isolate the effects of one variable on another.

Before discussing the means of achieving this control it is perhaps useful to take an example of an experiment in which several types of extraneous variable come to light. Consider a hypothetical experiment designed to compare the effectiveness of two communications which differ only in the characteristics of the presumed source. Let us assume that in this experiment two groups of subjects are exposed to the same warning on the dangers of pollution, but that the first group is told that the warning comes from an eminent ecologist, whereas the second group is told that the author is an eminent linguist. The independent variable is thus the degree to which the source is perceived as being 'informed', while the dependent variable might be the subject's concern about pollution. Let us now suppose that a reliable and valid measure of the dependent variable is taken after the communication, and the first

* It is simpler at this stage to consider the experiments in which only one independent variable is manipulated. However, 'multifactorial' experiments are also possible, and these will be discussed in a later section.

group is found to be significantly more concerned about pollution than the second group. Can we now conclude that the perceived source of the message is responsible for the difference between the two groups of subjects, or could some other variable account for the results? A number of questions may well spring to mind:

Were the two groups equivalent in their attitudes towards pollution at the beginning of the experiment?

Were the two groups composed of similar individuals with regard to age, sex, and other variables that may affect persuasibility?

Were the two messages identical in every respect apart from apparent authorship?

Were the two groups tested in similar conditions? For example was the experimenter's manner, time of day, type of surroundings the same for both?

Such questions concern the degree to which the relevant extraneous variables were controlled or held constant during the manipulation of the independed variable. If any of the extraneous variables were not properly controlled, for example if group one was treated more seriously than group two, it would be impossible to specify the cause of the difference between the groups. It might have been the type of source, or the seriousness of the treatment, or a combination of both factors that caused the difference in 'concern about pollution'. When an experiment leads to ambiguous conclusions of this sort it is said to be *confounded*. Hence confounding occurs whenever an extraneous variable is operating on the subjects at the same time as the independent variable so that either factor could be responsible for differences in the dependent variable.

If we wish to avoid confounding we must rigorously control all extraneous variables that could conceivably influence the subject's performance, leaving the field open, as it were, for the effects of the independent variable. The previous example may serve to demonstrate the magnitude of the problem and the range of extraneous variables that could, in principle, be operating in a single study. Broadly speaking these may be classified as follows:

Situational variables. All aspects of the experimental procedure and the environment that might influence the dependent variable. For example in the 'communication' experiment it would have been wise to control: manner of experimenter, time of day, features of the message, type of instructions and so forth.

Subject variables. All those characteristics of the subjects which might influence the dependent variable. Again in the previous experiment such variables as: persuasibility, age, sex, intelligence, initial attitudes to pollution, and education should be controlled.

Sequential variables. When subjects serve under two or more conditions of an experiment which are to be compared with each other the *order* of performance may influence the dependent variable. This type of extraneous variable will be illustrated in the next section.

EXERCISING CONTROL OVER EXTRANEOUS VARIABLES

In this section we shall classify the main techniques underlying the control of extraneous variables. We should emphasise at the outset however that not all extraneous variables can be effectively controlled within the time and resources generally available, and some selection of relevant variables must be made. This selection may make use of previous studies which have revealed the sort of extraneous variables likely to influence the behaviour under study. But in the final analysis it is a matter of individual judgment as to which of the many variables operating on the subjects at the time of the experiment may be safely ignored.

The most satisfactory level of control consists of the *elimination* of extraneous variables from the experimental situation altogether. Thus in an experiment to compare subjects' sensitivities to red and green light it may be decided to conduct the research in a sound-proof cubicle hence eliminating the disturbing effects of auditory stimuli on visual performance. It must be clear however that very few situational variables can be sensibly eliminated in social research. For example, it is not meaningful to talk of eliminating environmental temperature, or the time of day, or the personality of the experimenter. All these variables must necessarily impinge on the subject during an experimental session.

If these situational variables cannot be eliminated they can at least be held constant for all subjects throughout the experiment. Hence one can control such situational variables as experimenter characteristics, instructions, environmental factors, stimulus characteristics and so on by simply selecting one value of each characteristic (i.e. a particular experimenter, a typewritten set of instructions, a particular room temperature, humidity and noise level, etc.) and holding these constant throughout the experiment. The *method of constancy* also provides effective control for many subject variables. For example if age and intelligence are extraneous variables thought to influence the dependent variable they can be held constant by selecting only those subjects who fall within a specific narrow age and intelligence bracket. However this form of control of subject variables does limit the generalisability of the results. If an informed source is found to change attitudes more effectively than an uninformed source, and the findings are based on observations with thirty-year-old subjects, it does not follow that the relationship will also apply to teenagers or forty-year-olds.

Probably the most common form of control, at least for subject variables, is known as matching. This does not attempt to hold the extraneous variables completely constant—which is not always feasible—but simply to ensure that the variation in each extraneous variable is the same at each level of the independent variable.*
Thus it might not be possible or desirable to run our communication experiment exclusively on thirty-year-olds. Provided we can balance the age variable by ensuring a similar distribution of ages in the two experimental groups (those exposed to the informed and uninformed source) there is no chance that age will be confounded with the independent variable—type of source. The same principle

---

* When an independent variable is manipulated it takes on different values in each experimental condition. The term *level* is used to refer to these different values. Hence the minimum number of levels which constitutes manipulation of the independent variable is two e.g. informed versus uninformed source, red light versus green light, etc.

may be applied to situational variables; thus if several experimenters are used in a particular study one should ensure that the proportion of subjects tested by each experimenter is the same at each level of the independent variable (see Fig. 4.1).

Independent variable

Level I (e.g. Red stimulus)	Level II (e.g. Green stimulus)
10 subjects tested by experimenter 1	10 subjects tested by experimenter 1
5 subjects tested by experimenter 2	5 subjects tested by experimenter 2
8 subjects tested by experimenter 3	8 subjects tested by experimenter 3

Fig. 4.1 The control of a situational variable (experimenter effects) by matching.

A fourth method of control—known as *randomisation*—is useful when all other methods fail. Human behaviour is influenced by such a wide range of extraneous variables—the weather; time of day; noise; the subject's motivational state, physical state, past experience, financial problems, personal relationships and so on—that we could hardly expect to be able to eliminate, hold constant, or balance out all of these variables. Indeed many of them would pose major problems of measurement quite apart from the difficulties of strict control. A partial solution to this problem is to assign subjects randomly to each condition in the experiment so that in the long run any differences between conditions will cancel out. Of course this method of control does not work perfectly. We can only be confident about the similarity between our groups of subjects when very large numbers have been randomly assigned to each condition. The smaller the groups the more likely it is that some differences will not cancel out even after randomisation. Nevertheless it is possible to make allowance for this random variation between groups when our data is statistically analysed. Provided the allocation of subjects to experimental conditions has been random the statistical test will automatically assess whether group differences on the dependent variable can be explained entirely on the basis of random fluctuation. If not, the implication is that the independent variable is responsible for the variations in the dependent variable.

Of course it is not possible to control situational variables by the random allocation of subjects to each treatment. If we wish to control for the disturbing effects of noise or some similar variable, and the previous techniques are not feasible, then *randomising the order* in which we run subjects from each group is advisable. Hence one would not test all the subjects exposed to an informed source before those exposed to an uninformed source, or vice versa, but one would randomise the order in which subjects from each condition were tested. In this way any environmental effects occurring through time would be expected to cancel out across the two conditions.

Finally, mention should be made of a very powerful technique for controlling subject variables known as the *single group* or *repeated-measures* design. In this type of experiment all the subjects receive the various treatments rather than having different groups tested under each condition. Hence one might test a group of subjects' reaction times to red light, followed by the *same* group's responses to green light. In this way one controls all the genetic and environmental properties of the subjects leaving only the situational variables to be controlled in other ways. This is clearly superior to the random division of subjects into groups since it actually guarantees the creation of identical groups for each treatment rather than relying on chance. On the other hand the single group design is vulnerable to an additional extraneous variable; one has to assume that experience in one condition will not influence the group's performance in later conditions. That is, sequential effects become important when the same group is tested under each level of the independent variable.

Sequential effects can be controlled by *counterbalancing* the order in which the treatments are assigned. For example in comparing reactions to red and green light we could arrange to have half the subjects tested in the order red-green and the other half in the order green-red. In this way we might expect any sequence effects, due to practice, familiarisation or whatever, to cancel out across the two conditions. This assumption is reasonable in the case of colour effects on reaction time, but it is less plausible when applied to more complex types of social enquiry. Suppose, for example, an experimenter is investigating the effect of group pressure on decision making. He sets up two treatment conditions. In one (T_1) each subject is required to judge the size of an object after hearing a group of his fellows (actually stooges) consistently underestimate the size; in the second condition (T_2) the subject is required to make the same judgments in isolation. The experimenter decides to control for individual differences (subject variables) by using the same subjects in each condition. He controls sequential effects by counterbalancing the order in which subjects are tested, half do T_1–T_2 and half do T_2–T_1. Now if counterbalancing is to be effective we must assume that the influence of T_1 on T_2 is the same as the influence of T_2 on T_1, but this is far from certain. It seems much more likely that after group pressure to underestimate (T_1) subjects would tend to underestimate even in isolation (T_2), whereas subjects who did T_2 first would be *less* likely to underestimate when transferred to the group situation. Thus the two types of transfer effect might operate in different directions tending to camouflage or reduce the real difference between the treatments. Obviously in this sort of experiment the random division of subjects into two groups would be safer than adopting a counterbalanced single groups design.

It is difficult to make any general recommendations about the relative usefulness of the various control techniques. Each has its advantages and disadvantages depending on the aims of the experimenter and the resources—time, money and subjects—which are available to him. Thus it is generally useful to hold intelligence constant when conducting educational experiments, but not if the results of the study are to be applied at all levels of educational ability. In this situation balancing intelligence would be a more appropriate control technique. It is often desirable to match groups

75

for age, sex, education and occupational status in social research but this is only feasible with a very large subject pool and the resources to investigate large numbers of potential subjects in order to complete the 'quota' for each level of the extraneous variables. Such examples could be extended indefinitely, but in the final analysis the researcher must learn for himself how to relate control decisions to the aims and resources behind each study. To help in this task we have summarised in Table 4.1 the main techniques of control, their applicability, advantages and disadvantages.

TABLE 4.1   THE PROPERTIES OF CONTROL TECHNIQUES

Control technique	Class of extraneous variables to which applicable	Advantages and disadvantages
Elimination	Some situational variables (e.g. noise)	Very limited applicability.
Method of constancy	Situational variables (e.g. intructions, room temperature)	Allows complete control of situational variables, but not always feasible.
	Subject variables (e.g. age, sex)	Allows complete control, but limits generality of findings.
Matching	Subject variables (e.g. age, sex)	Allows complete control, does not limit generality, and permits examination of subject variable effects. But it can only be used on one or two variables unless very large subject populations are available.
	Situational variables (e.g. experimenter effects)	Allows complete control but not always feasible.
Randomisation (of subjects to treatments)	Subject variables (e.g. age, sex)	Does not produce perfect control and depends on large numbers of subjects. But useful for residual subject variables which are not controllable in any other way (or may not be recognised).

	Situational variables (e.g. noise)	Allows partial control of randomly occurring events beyond the experimenter's control.
Repeated measures design	Subject variables (e.g. age, sex, intelligence)	Allows complete control of all possible subject variables but introduces sequence effects.
Counter-balancing	Sequence effects (e.g. fatigue, sensitisation)	Allows complete control of any sequence effect provided these are the same between all treatments.

THE CONTROL OF THE INDEPENDENT VARIABLE

The second facet of experimental control is the purposive manipulation of the independent variable in such a way as to reveal its effects on the dependent variable. The technique used to do this is normally referred to as the *experimental design*. In our previous discussions a rather simple design was used as a basis for illustrating the various methods of controlling the extraneous variables. This was the *randomised-two-groups design* in which two groups of subjects are exposed to different levels of the independent variable (say red and green light) and the resulting differences in the dependent variable (say reaction time) are examined. There are, in fact, a large number of different designs for manipulating the independent variable (or variables) in an experiment, and these will be reviewed in this section. The discussion has been limited to a rather general account of the main types of design used in social and behavioural research. For a more detailed analysis of these designs, together with the appropriate statistical procedures, the reader should consult other sources.[9]

SINGLE FACTOR DESIGNS

As indicated above the simplest method of examining the effect of one variable on another is to randomly allocate subjects to various groups and then expose these groups to different levels of the independent variable. The previous examples involved two levels of the independent variable, and correspondingly, two groups of experimental subjects,* but this design can be readily extended to more than two conditions. Suppose, for example, an experimenter wished to assess the effect of reward on the rate at which subjects learn a particular task. He might well decide that several different levels of reward should be investigated, say 0, 2, 4, 8, and 16p per each correct response. He would therefore divide his subjects randomly into five separate groups, each of which would be tested under one level of the independent variable. This is a *single-factor* design because only *one* independent variable, or factor, is being manipulated—reward. The design may be represented diagrammatically as in Fig. 4.2.

Independent variable

Treatment levels	1	2	3	4	....	k
Subject groups	Grp I	Grp II	Grp III	Grp IV	....	Grp K

Fig. 4.2   Single factor design—randomised groups.

The assumption underlying this design is that individual differences between subjects will more or less cancel out if the subjects are assigned to the various groups at random (see p. 73). Hence the average performance (mean) of each group should be the same at the beginning of the experiment, although this is not normally measured. Any difference on the dependent variable emerging at the end of the experiment can then be ascribed to the differential effects of the k treatments, providing, of course, the relevant extraneous variables have been controlled.

---

* It often happens that one group of subjects is exposed to a positive level of the independent variable (e.g. group pressure) while the second group receives a 'zero' level of the independent variable (e.g. no pressure). Under these conditions the second group is normally referred to as the *control* group.

It is sometimes suggested that the equivalence of the groups should be checked before the experiment by conducting a *pre-test* of performance on the dependent variable. This is sometimes useful for the experimenter's peace of mind, but it is apt to introduce more complications than it is worth. For example, a pre-test may alert subjects to the presence of an experiment and this may result in high motivation for all groups, thereby masking the effects of the main treatments. Ross and Smith[10] have analysed the consequences of pre-testing in single factor designs and conclude that 'it often is better *not* to pre-test' except where one is interested in the effects of the independent variable on individual subjects, or where the original groups were not randomly selected and some check on equivalence is required.

The statistical analysis of such designs is based on the important principle of *analysis of variance*. In order to establish a significant relationship between independent and dependent variables it is necessary to show that the differences between group means are too large to be attributed to random fluctuation in the data. This is done by comparing the variations between group means with the variaton between subjects *within* each group. The first type of variation (between groups) will reflect the operation of the independent variable, whereas the second type of variation (within groups) will reflect chance differences between individual subjects. By comparing the two we can assess whether the differences between the group means are greater than could be expected on the basis of individual differences alone. If they are we can conclude that the independent variable is having a significant effect on performance quite apart from the random fluctuations one would expect by chance in any set of group means.

Analysis of variance is thus an extremely powerful technique* for teasing out the causes or variation in a set of observations arising from experimental designs. It does not however reveal the precise relationship between independent and dependent variables. Its

---

* The *power* of a statistical test refers to its ability to detect a significant effect when one is present in the data.

function is merely to determine whether a particular factor is causing variation in the dependent variable. If, however, one is predicting a particular pattern of effects, for example that learning rate in each group will be proportional to the level of reward, then a more powerful variation of the basic technique should be employed.[11] Equally if the experimenter wishes to test for a difference between two specific groups selected from the set of k, additional analysis will be required after the general analysis of variance has been completed.[12] Thus the main purpose of the technique is simply to indicate whether there is any relationship at all between the value of the independent variable and the behaviour of the subjects.

The value of single-factor designs

The single factor design provides a convenient method of analysing the effect of one variable on another. It is frequently used in psychological and educational research to investigate in some detail how an isolated relationship between two variables behaves. For example, one might wish to study the relationship between fatigue and problem solving ability, or compare the effectiveness of four different teaching methods, or find the precise relationship between competitiveness and group size. These, and many more problems, could be set up as single-factor experiments and some sort of conclusion could be reached. But as we have already argued real-life phenomena usually depend on much more complex interactions between variables than is represented by this basic experimental design. One could not make very accurate predictions about teaching efficiency merely from a knowledge of the formal teaching method being applied. Many facets of pupil ability, teacher characteristics and school environment would have to be considered first. And so it is with most other fields of social and psychological activity. Hence single-factor designs are only a first step in mapping out the complex pattern of interactions underlying most of the human behaviour we would wish to study.

FACTORIAL DESIGNS

In a factorial design the experimenter is able to manipulate two or more independent variables simultaneously and to observe their separate and joint effects on the dependent variable. As in the single-factor design subjects are randomly allocated to the various experimental treatments but each treatment consists of the joint occurrence of one level of each factor in the experiment. For example the experimenter may be interested in the effects of fatigue and illumination on problem solving ability. He might choose to manipulate fatigue at three levels (high, medium and low) and illumination at two levels (bright and dim). Now in a factorial design 3×2 experimental groups would be set up; viz., each treatment would consist of the joint action of one fatigue level and one brightness level so that all possible combinations were covered. This particular *two factor* design is represented in Fig. 4.3.

		Independent variable (factor) I Fatigue		
		High	*Medium*	*Low*
Independent variable (factor) II	Bright	Grp 1	Grp 2	Grp 3
Illumination	Dim	Grp 4	Grp 5	Grp 6

Fig. 4.3   Factorial design: Two-factor, randomised groups.

In principle this design could be extended to include many additional factors, but the practical demand for extra subjects and the theoretical problems of analysis and interpretation become more or less prohibitive above four or five factors. (e.g. a four-factor design with 3 levels per factor requires $3^4 = 81$ groups of subjects).

The assumption underlying randomised factorial designs is identical to the one discussed in connection with single factor experiments. As all the subjects are allocated randomly to each treatment combination the various groups are taken as equivalent on the dependent variable at the beginning of the experiment. The difference in group means observed at the end of the experiment are then interpreted in terms of the effects of the independent variables. But the factorial design not only allows us to examine the main effect of each independent variable on the dependent variable, it also has the great advantage (relative to a series of separate single-factor experiments) of revealing the interactive effects of several factors working together.

Let us take as an example the problem-solving experiment just cited. The data from this experiment should provide the answers to the following three questions:

1. Does fatigue influence performance?
2. Does level of illumination influence performance?
3. Is the effect of fatigue the same at each level of illumination? (Or what amounts to the same question: Is the effect of illumination the same at each level of fatigue?)

It is the third question about the *interaction* between the independent variables which is the distinctive, important feature of factorial designs. The reason for emphasising it is that many social phenomena cannot be adequately understood without considering interactions between causal effects. Even in the simple example above it seems highly plausible that an interaction might occur; for example we might expect the effect of fatigue to be *more* marked under dull conditions of illumination than under bright conditions. Such relationships could not be examined by any number of single-factor experiments, but factorial designs provide a powerful and efficient method for coping with them. Even where interaction effects fail to emerge it should not be thought that the factorial design has been wasted. In the first place the use of factorial designs need not involve any sacrifice in terms of the precision with which the main effects are evaluated. That is, no improvement in precision could be achieved if the entire sample of subjects were placed in a single-factor design. Secondly, the findings of zero interaction is useful in itself, since it means that the effect of each main factor is stable across a range of levels of the other factor or factors. Thus a zero interaction effect in the problem solving experiment would mean that the effect of fatigue on performance is more or less the same across a range of different lighting conditions.

The statistical treatment of factorial designs is operationally complex though it depends on the relatively simple concepts underlying analysis of variance. In the case of two-factor analyses* there are four sources of variation in the data:

1. Factor I effects (e.g. the difference *between* grp means 1, 2. and 3 in Fig. 4.3)
2. Factor II effects (e.g. the difference *between* grp means 1 and 4 in Fig. 4.3)
3. Interaction effects (e.g. the difference *between* (Grp Mean 1— Grp Mean 2) and (Grp Mean 4—Grp Mean 5)
4. Chance fluctuations between subjects (e.g. the differences between subjects' scores *within* any group)

To determine whether any of the first three effects are significant one asks the question: is the variation between the relevant set of group means greater than one would expect on the basis of chance variations between subjects (as measured under 4)? If so, that particular effect is said to be significant.

Whilst the answer to the above question depends on a relatively complex analysis of variance it is often possible to gain a preliminary insight into the various effects by graphical representations of the group means. By way of illustration we have prepared five hypothetical graphs to represent different possible outcomes to the problem solving experiment. In each case the mean problem solving scores (the dependent variable) are represented on the ordinate of the graph, and the values of the independent variable I (fatigue) on the abscissa. Two lines are then drawn, one for each level of the second independent variable (illumination). Naturally

---

* In higher order designs (e.g. 3 or 4 factors) there are many more interactions to be considered.

the representations of the independent variable could have been reversed on the graphs.

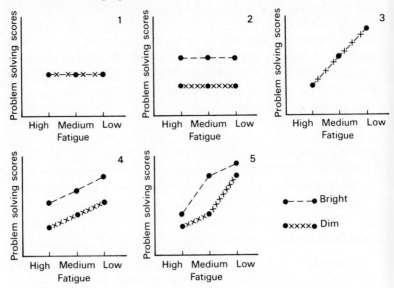

Fig. 4.4   Some of the possible outcomes of a two-factor experiment.

Having drawn out the results in this way it is often possible to predict the results of the analysis of variance with a good deal of precision. Thus in 1 we would not expect fatigue or illumination to be found significant. In 2 illumination is apparently having a significant effect on performance, but fatigue appears irrelevant. In 3, fatigue is operative and illumination appears to be ineffective. In 4, both illumination and fatigue are influencing performance. And finally in 5 both factors are again significant and there appears to be a significant interaction as well; that is, fatigue is operative at both levels of illumination but the pattern of its influence varies according to whether the illumination is bright or dim. Of course experimental data does not always fall neatly into one of these patterns but the graphing of results is still invariably a useful key to the understanding of one's results.

MATCHED-GROUP DESIGNS

In our previous discussion of single-factor and multi-factor designs the main technique for controlling subject variables was randomisation. This is a quick, convenient and simple method of control but it suffers from two disadvantages. First, the control is not perfect, though as we have seen statistical methods will take account of random differences between experimental groups. Secondly, and this is the important point, the variability between the scores in each group will be relatively high because a wide range of subject characteristics will be included. Hence when it comes to conducting analyses of variance it will be rather difficult to show that the group means are significantly different from each other relative to the variation within each group. In other words if the effects of the experimental treatments are weak (i.e. not very marked) a randomised groups design may be too insensitive to pick up the differences between groups.

One method of reducing the variation within each group of subjects is to use a matched-group design. Instead of randomly allocating subjects to each level of the independent variable we divide them into a number of homogeneous groups on the basis of a subject variable thought to influence performance. Each group is then spread randomly across all experimental conditions as shown in Fig. 4.5 for a single-factor experiment.[13]

| | | \multicolumn{6}{c}{*Independent variable* *Treatment levels*} |
		1	2	3	4	....	k
	I						
Subject	II						
groups	III						
	IV						

Fig. 4.5 Single-factor design: matched groups.

This procedure is no more than was previously described under the topic of control by matching, but we are now in a better position to understand its significance in relation to randomised designs. Consider, for example, the hypothetical experiment on learning rate as a function of reward. There were five different levels of reward and, using a randomised design, it was necessary to show that the variation between the learning scores in these five conditions was greater than one would expect on the basis of individual variation within each group. Now let us assume that learning rate is also heavily dependent on a subject's IQ. Since IQ has been controlled by randomisation we can expect a very large variation in performance *within* each group, sufficient perhaps to mask the effect of the various treatments. Under a matched-group design one could overcome this problem by dividing the subjects into, say, three groups according to IQ (High, Medium, Low) and then performing the entire experiment *within* each IQ group. The design is shown in Fig. 4.6,

Independent Variable—Reward

		0	2	4	8	16
Subject	High IQ					
groups	Medium IQ					
	Low IQ					

Fig. 4.6   Single-factor design: matched groups.

where each cell contains the same number of subjects. The advantage of this design is that random variation can now be assessed from the difference between subjects *within* each reward-IQ combined treatment. This measure of random variation will inevitably be less than the one that would have been obtained by allowing IQ to vary in each experimental group. Hence we are now in a better position to detect small variations in learning rate as a function of reward.

There are several ways in which subjects may be matched across treatments in this sort of design. The subjects may actually be tested on some variable known to influence the dependent variable (e.g. IQ in the above example) and then divided into homogeneous groups on this basis. Each group is then randomly subdivided between the treatments. A more perfect matching is obtained by having each subject matched with himself (i.e. each subject performs each treatment condition). This is known as a repeated measures design and raises problems of sequencing the treatments (see p. 74). Finally in sociological and educational research it is common to find natural groupings of subjects which provide a useful basis for matching. Hence pupils within a particular school are usually more homogeneous with regard to a wide range of intellectual and social variables than pupils selected from different schools. The same applies to neighbourhoods, professional groups, families and so forth. In these cases it is often useful to match subjects on one of these criteria, and then to randomly allocate the subjects within each matched group to each of the treatment levels.

In formal terms the structure of a single-factor design with matched groups is identical to a factorial design with two independent variables. The variable on which subjects are matched simply replaces the second factor of the factorial design (hence figs. 4.3 and 4.5 are structurally similar). The difference between the two is that the variable used for matching is not of interest in itself, that is as a potential influence on the dependent variable, but is introduced simply as a means of reducing the variability of the observations within each treatment combination, thereby improving the sensitivity of the design to the effects of the main factor. Nevertheless a matched-groups design is treated statistically in much the same way as a factorial design so that the end result is a statement of the relationships between the dependent variable and (1) the independent variable acting in isolation, (2) the matching variable acting in isolation, and (3) the independent and matching variables acting simultaneously. But since the matching variable is not *manipulated* experimentally, only by selection, it is not possible to interpret its relationships with the dependent variable (i.e. 2 and 3) in causal terms.

The researcher is often faced with a choice between matching and randomisation as a method of control. There is little doubt that subject variables are more accurately controlled by matching, but there is no point in doing this if the matching variable is irrelevant to the subjects' performance. There would be no reason to match subjects on height, for example, in our learning experiment. Not only would this be unnecessary, it would be disadvantageous because the statistical constraints inherent in a matched-groups design make it more difficult to reach significance. It is only when the matching variable is highly correlated with the dependent variable that its use can be expected to reduce withingroup variation sufficiently to highlight the differences between treatments and offset the statistical costs involved in matching. In short one should only use a matched-groups design where there is a good chance of extracting a large amount of what would otherwise be uncontrolled variation from one's data.[14]

ANALYSIS OF COVARIANCE

A matched-groups design is often impracticable even though it may be the most effective method of experimental control. For example in educational research it is often desirable to match for intelligence when comparing the effect of different instructional techniques on academic achievement. However it may be inconvenient or impossible to collect homogeneous IQ groups for subdivision among the experimental treatments. If, in such circumstances, the extraneous variable is known to be highly correlated with performance, control by randomisation may render the design insensitive (i.e. the variation within each treatment condition may be large enough to mask the differences between treatment). This is the sort of problem that would arise if there were large variations in intelligence within each treatment condition of an educational experiment.

Analysis of covariance is a technique for removing the effects of an extraneous variable statistically when experimental control is impractical or inconvenient. Provided the score of each subject on the extraneous variable is known, the subjects can be assigned to the treatment conditions randomly and an adjustment can be made for effects of the extraneous variable at the stage of analysis. Hence the purpose of the procedure is very similar to that of matching; the aim is to extract the effect of the extraneous variable from the data and thereby permit a clearer view of the treatment effects. In this way weaker main effects can be detected in educational experiments by using as a yardstick the variation within an homogeneous IQ group rather than the variation in a group of mixed IQ levels. In analysis of covariance this extra sensitivity is provided by statistical rather than experimental means.

Analysis of covariance is thus not a design itself, but rather a technique for analysis which can be used with most single-factor and multi-factor designs provided the scores on a relevant extraneous variable are available. It is even possible to decide to use the method after the experiment, for example if a normal analysis of variance is too insensitive and the experimenter knows that the effects of an important subject variable could be extracted from the data. In fact analysis of covariance is generally more efficient at 'purifying' the experimental data than a matched-groups design, and it is certainly more likely to be feasible.

The main argument against the use of analysis of covariance, apart from the computational burden, is that it does not permit the analysis of interaction effects between the extraneous variable and the independent variable(s), whereas a matched-groups design does. Hence, to return to the educational experiment, if intelligence is controlled by matching, it will be possible to determine *(a)* the effect of different instructional techniques, *(b)* the effect of intelligence and *(c)* whether the effect of instructional techniques is the same at each level of intelligence. It is this third, interaction, effect which is likely to be important in many educational and social research fields. If intelligence is controlled by randomisation and an analysis of covariance is subsequently computed there will be no way of investigating this type of interaction.

To sum up, analysis of covariance is a useful means of overcoming the insensitivity of a randomised design without resorting to the experimental labour of a matched-groups design. It is convenient to use, and efficient, but it does not provide as much information as a factorial design in which a matching variable is treated as one of the experimental factors.

EXPERIMENTAL DESIGNS INVOLVING CONFOUNDING

Generally speaking the more complex the phenomena under study the more variables must be included in the explanatory model. Simple aspects of behaviour like signal detection, or visual reaction time, may be examined realistically in terms of three or four main independent variables but topics like leadership behaviour, social perception and so forth, require a multi-variate approach of a much higher order. As soon as we begin to consider complex factorial designs the number of treatment combinations becomes unworkably large. A study of attitude change in which the characteristics of the source, communication, and receiver are each to be manipulated at, say, four different levels would require a factorial design of sixty-four treatments combinations. If all the interactions and main effects are to be examined at least 128 subjects will be required. If additional factors or levels are added to the experiment the number of treatment combinations will increase geometrically.

A wide range of experimental designs has been developed to enable researchers to deal with these multi-factorial designs without paying the excessive cost in subjects of a complete factorial design. The technique used is to omit certain treatment combinations, but to do this in such a way that the main effects and important interactions are still examinable. Hence one may undertake a matched-groups design in which the number of subjects within each group is insufficient to cover all treatment combinations. By allocating the subjects within each matched group to appropriate treatments the most important effects may still be assessed but some information about high-order interactions will be lost. These interactions are said to be *confounded* because they cannot be separated from the effects of other factors, in this case the effects of the matching variable.

Many other designs are available to enable the experimenter to reduce experimental costs (in time and subjects) by sacrificing some precision in examining the effects of interactions or extraneous variables. The procedures are too complex to describe here,[15] but they are mentioned in order to emphasise the flexibility of experimental methods even in multi-factorial situations.

GENERALISABILITY OF EXPERIMENTAL FINDINGS

Despite the efficiency of experimental methods in teasing out causal relations between variables, it should not be forgotten that the generalisability of experimental findings to other situations is limited in much the same way as any other social research technique. It is conventional to emphasise the need to sample subjects randomly from the population of individuals to whom one intends to generalise. This is certainly an important consideration, but the same principle applies to every aspect of an experiment from the sampling of treatments to the sampling of experimenters and the sampling of criterion measures. Strictly speaking the findings of any experiment are limited to that particular set of subjects, experimenters, temperatures, measurement techniques, hours of the day, etc., which defined the context of the experiment. The only basis for generalising to other subjects, experimenters, temperatures and so on, is random sampling. That is to say, if the experimenters used in any particular study were randomly selected from the population of, say, British experimenters we would then be justified in generalising our results to other hypothetical experimenters. A similar argument applies to each of the myriad of variables which might have feasibly influenced the outcome of our experiment.

Now this limitation on generalisability raises obvious problems since we can hardly sample more than a few variables in any particular experiment. Factors like temperature, lighting, experimenter, and time of day are usually held constant either for convenience or out of sheer necessity. Does this mean that our findings are rigidly tied to the exact circumstances of the experiment? The answer clearly depends on whether these factors could be expected to influence the relationship between the dependent and independent variables. It is often a matter of intuition whether a particular variable can be ignored for the purposes of generalisation, and the judgment clearly depends on the type of behaviour being investigated. Hence the study of fairly basic psychological or physiological responses, like reflex actions, can reasonably be generalised to the population at large even though a few subjects were selected possibly on a non-random basis. The point is that a subject's reactions to electric shocks or pinpricks are unlikely to vary with intelligence, height or occupational status. In the same way the personality of experimenter is unlikely to influence a subject's performance in an experiment on auditory perception, but it might be crucial in a study of social interaction or decision-making.[16] In these circumstances an effort should be made to sample a range of 'experimenter types' and to include this variable as a factor in the experiment. If the experimenter variable is then shown to have no effect on performance one can safely generalise the findings to a wide range of testing situations. Hence in any experimental study one's findings are specific to the circumstances of the design except in so far as:

1. the variables have been randomly sampled from the populations of interest (subjects, tasks, experimenters, etc.) and shown to have no effect on the relationship between dependent and independent variable;

2. it is known from past experimentation that 1 is the case;

3. it is intuitively obvious that the experimental findings are independent of particular research circumstances.

LABORATORY EXPERIMENTS AND FIELD EXPERIMENTS

A great deal has been said about the differences and relative merits of laboratory and field experiments as though they were two separate techniques of social enquiry. In fact there is no fundamental difference between a study conducted in a laboratory and one which takes place in a school, hospital or some other social setting. Provided the logic of experimental methods is satisfied, provided the independent variable is actively manipulated, the extraneous variables controlled, the subjects assigned to treatments at random, and the dependent variable adequately measured, there will be no problem in establishing the causal connections between the variables under study. Apart from the practical difficulty of meeting these criteria, there are no real differences between field experiments and research laboratory experiments. There is, however, often a difference in the degree to which experimental findings can be generalised from the research findings. In field research it is often impossible to hold extraneous variables constant and they must be controlled by randomisation rather than one of the tighter methods like elimination, or the method of constancy. For example, in a field experiment on the effects of worker participation on productivity it would hardly be possible to hold the past history of the industrial units constant, or the personality of the supervisors, or the physical working conditions, and so on. Now provided a number of industrial organisations are assigned at random to the different levels of the independent variable—worker participation—these extraneous variables will be expected to cancel out in the long run due to randomisation. In a laboratory study we might have found more effective means of control and been able to hold such factors constant. The consequences of these differences are *(a)* that significance will be harder to attain in a field experiment because the random fluctuation between treatments will be greater and *(b)* by way of compensation, if significance is obtained it will be more widely generalisable to other situations because many of the extraneous variables will have been 'sampled' across a relatively wide range.

In summary then, field experiments tend to be less tightly controlled than laboratory studies in the sense that extraneous variables are controlled more often by randomisation. As a consequence significance will be harder to attain but more readily generalisable to other situations. As in all other aspects of experimental design the researcher's choice of approach will be determined by the nature of his problem (pure or applied, general or specific, etc.), and the resources he has available (time, money, subject cooperation, etc.). In this chapter we have attempted to spell out the consequences of different design strategies on the precision and validity of one's conclusions. Hopefully the experimenter will be able to use these principles to achieve his own research aims as intelligently and efficiently as possible.

Strategy and choice

In this final chapter we try to stand back a little from the technicalities of research design and consider some of the more fundamental decisions the researcher has to make when planning his investigation. We are concerned with *(a)* the basis for choosing a particular problem; *(b)* the formulation of research objectives; and *(c)* the selection of theoretical and methodological approaches. These are not necessarily neat steps along which the researcher progresses towards his goal. Nor are they meant to describe the way research workers actually behave, as there are patently as many different ways to plan research as there are researchers to do the planning. We feel, however, that the standards of research could be improved if planning decisions were made *consciously* and with some appreciation of the risks and consequences associated with the various alternatives. The researcher who 'drifts into' his investigation with little understanding of the decisions he is implicitly making cannot expect to achieve his objectives with the degree of validity, economy and accuracy that would otherwise be possible.

THE CHOICE OF TOPIC

The first and most daunting problem is that of choosing a topic for research and defining its boundaries. The step is an obvious one, but we know surprisingly little about how it is done, and even less about the criteria for arriving at a feasible and potentially fruitful research problem.

There are a number of obvious, though frequently neglected, external constraints; thus, the choice of topic is often dictated by available finance. A researcher with meagre funds will be unable to undertake a large-scale, or long-duration exercise, which certain topics require. The idea, for example, of studying the psychological aspects of child development in several cultures with the aid of representative samples drawn into a longitudinal design could only be entertained by a researcher who was able to command funds to engage several teams of workers over a long period of time.

Not unrelated to the question of funds, are the particular values and orientations evinced by those granting financial support for a research project. These often take the form of a demand for particular applied problems to be answered, but an ingenious researcher can often design a study which will meet these practical requirements while extending our understanding of important theoretical issues. There are a number of American market-research studies, designed to assess the popularity and impact of a particular product, which also produced theoretical insights into the psychology of human motivation.

Finally, the academic researcher usually works within the limits of his own field of expertise, which means that he cannot easily investigate broad, interdisciplinary fields such as the basis of 'industrial productivity' or 'race relations', though he can work on specific aspects of them. To cope with such complex issues as the 'causes of racial tension' large interdisciplinary research teams containing psychologists, sociologists, demographers, political scientists, and other social scientists are beginning to emerge. The individual researcher is therefore more likely to produce worthwhile results by working in a fairly restricted field which does not involve the interaction of many different disciplines.

In addition to such external constraints the choice of problem will also be influenced by the cultural and political climate within which the researcher works,[1] thereby defining a 'pool' of acceptable research problems from which a choice must be made. It is at this point that guidance is most frequently needed in choosing a potentially fruitful field for research. The choice should be determined, at least in part, by the following considerations:

1. The extent to which a piece of research will break new ground or fill a gap in an existing body of knowledge.
2. Whether the problem is scientifically testable; that is, are there relevant and attainable observations which could be used to support or falsify the theories involved?
3. The applicability of the results to the solution of practical problems.
4. The cost of the research relative to its potential value and importance.

This last point brings us to the critical question of assessing the potential importance of research over and above its mere feasibility. While there will always be a need for competent, routine investigations which extend and amplify an established field of research, there is certainly also a need for far-reaching, creative research which brings together within one theoretical framework a range of previously disparate facts. Unfortunately there is no known procedure for generating such original research problems, but we can at least try to assess the potential value of the research proposals we produce. The questions posed by Webb for the evaluation of psychological experiments are probably of general relevance to the social sciences;

> Very simply, this boils down to being able to evaluate the probable consequence of your findings with the question which goes something like this: 'In how many and what kind of specific circumstances will the relationships or rules that hold in this experiment hold in such other instances?' . . . . If the rule applies to what apparently is a vast heterogeneity of events in time and space, in varieties of species and surrounds, this rule is likely to have great value. Stated otherwise the extent to which our variables and situations are unique and rare in contrast to universal and common largely determines the extent to which the findings are likely to be considered trivial or tremendous in their implications.[2]

These, then, are some of the considerations which should be borne in mind when selecting a research problem, although it is obvious that very few topics will satisfy all these criteria. Many laboratory studies in psychology, for example, have very limited practical significance but pose challenging theoretical problems; on the other hand much survey research is undertaken largely because of its relevance to contemporary issues. The factors listed above are therefore only general guidelines for assessing research potential, and in any case do not actually assist the researcher in *generating* the research problem in the first place. This is largely a matter of intellectual curiosity applied to a realm of experience which the researcher cannot fully understand. Kerlinger says, 'The scientist will usually experience an obstacle to understanding, a vague unrest about observed and unobserved phenomena, a curiosity as to why something is as it is.'[3] This is the psychological origin of a research idea to which the criteria of feasibility, testability, practical significance, and potential contribution to theory should be subsequently applied.

THE FORMULATION OF OBJECTIVES

While the 'sensing' of a problem may be a matter of imagination and intuition, the scientific investigation of that problem is a more formal affair, depending on the exercise of logic, objectivity and control. It follows that a rather general, and perhaps vague, research problem will have to be translated into a more precise statement before it can be studied scientifically. Thus the problem 'What causes social unrest?' is too diffuse, in its present form, to permit investigation, whereas the more refined problem 'How are public attitudes influenced by the rate of inflation?' is sufficiently specific to serve as the object of a research study. By specifying objectives we ensure that there is no ambiguity about what is to be measured or what particular relationships between variables are to be tested.

Herbert Hyman's distinction between *descriptive and explanatory* objectives, although relating to survey design, is fundamental to all social research. In the descriptive study the object is 'precise measurement of one or more dependent variables in some defined population or sample of that population'.[4] The object in the explanatory study is to uncover the effects of independent variables, that is to test hypothesised causal relationships between variables. Putting this another way the descriptive study is the researcher's first reaction to a problem, an attempt to find more relevant facts, whereas the explanatory study is an attempt to solve the problem by testing an explicit hypothesis to explain the facts.

Thus descriptive studies may be necessary in many cases for the very formulation of hypotheses which are to form the basis of explanatory research. In order to develop hypotheses it is not economical to rely entirely on introspection and personal experience. To 'look around' the society in which one lives and to 'think about' the psychological problems one's friends or colleagues experience may supply us with useful insights into a possible research area, but these insights may often be quite spurious and unproductive. These ideas must therefore be screened, as Peter Blau suggests, by means of exploratory and descriptive quantitative data. Those which survive such *screening tests* are apt to be more correct than original speculations, as the hard facts often show unexpected relationships between variables and may thus challenge the initial imaginative but impressionistic conclusion reached by the researcher.[5] In a new field it is obviously more efficient to obtain some reliable descriptive data before finally selecting an hypothesis and investing time and resources in a thorough explanatory study. However when an area is more highly developed and a good deal of research has already taken place, it will be possible to deduce hypotheses from existing research results and to launch directly into further explanatory investigations.

It is sometimes suggested that a descriptive study may also be adapted for use as an explanatory, hypothesis-testing, device. Thus Hyman maintains that in the case of surveys 'the choice of a descriptive design permits the later test of a hypothesis by an approximation after the fact to an explanatory design, but the initial choice of an explanatory design precludes any later approximation to the design needed for a descriptive enquiry'.[6] The idea is that in the larger descriptive survey one can find subgroups with particular characteristics which can then be compared for explanatory purposes, whereas in the explanatory design one cannot subsequently combine the small specially selected samples to produce a valid general description of the universe of interest. Whilst the second half of this argument is obviously valid, the view that descriptive studies can be used both to suggest hypotheses *and* to test them is open to doubt. The problem is that in any large-scale descriptive study some of the apparent relationships between variables will have arisen by chance,* so that we can have little faith in an observed relationship unless it was predicted *in advance* on the basis of some theory or hypothesis. An unexpected relationship which emerges in a descriptive study should therefore be incorporated into hypotheses for subsequent *independent* testing and not accepted as valid on the basis of the same observations which suggested it in the first place.

This last point reflects the essential function of the hypothesis in science, which is to guide research by making predictive statements about what will happen to one variable when another variable changes. This is a much more powerful and efficient means of interpreting our environment than by simply observing what may be quite fortuitous relationships between events, and basing one's theories on these unpredicted relationships. The true test of understanding is to be able to predict what will happen (given knowledge of the antecedent conditions) rather than to explain what has happened after the event. It is by the systematic use of hypotheses that the scientist is protected from 'slipping back' into this simpler, but less efficient, mode of enquiry.

This belief in the power of hypotheses should not be mistaken however for 'hypothesis myopia', a term coined by Bachrach[7] to describe that condition in which the researcher becomes insensitive to any events outside the scope of the hypothesis. It certainly pays to consider all available observations, whether they are strictly

---

* The proportion of spuriously significant relationships will be approximately equal to the probability level used in assessing significance, normally 5 per cent. Hence in a study involving 100 independent correlations we would expect about 5 to be significant *by chance,* i.e. not really significant.

relevant to the hypothesis under test, in the hope of finding clues to new, and possibly more fundamental hypotheses. Our point is simply that the formal process of acquiring scientific knowledge depends on the formulation and rigorous testing of hypotheses; in addition there is every justification for capitalising on accidental observations and anomalous findings which suggest new hypotheses for investigation. Neither of these approaches should blind the researcher to the importance of the other.

To sum up this section, we have argued that the type of objective one adopts depends on the existing state of knowledge in the field. If there is little relevant knowledge, an exploratory study will be in order. If the researcher already has a good idea of the important variables in a problem area he is likely to conduct an explanatory study. In either case the defining of objectives is important because it helps to clarify and direct an investigation, and because by look-ing at the objectives it is possible to assess whether the problem is really manageable with available skills and resources. In the case of an explanatory study the objective takes the form of an hypothesis, or set of hypotheses, to be tested. These are, as it were, the tentative solutions to the problem, the researcher's method of explaining the facts. The hypothesis not only guides the researcher to investigate particular empirical relationships rather than random collections of facts, it also ensures by virtue of its predictive and testable nature that scientific knowledge is acquired efficiently and accurately.

There are, of course, good and bad hypotheses, just as there are good and bad research problems. Since the hypothesis is the tentative solution to a problem its value will be largely determined by the characteristics of the problem. We have already mentioned a set of criteria for a worthwhile research problem which may be briefly summarised as feasibility, applicability, testability, origin-ality, and generality. To this should be added parsimony, relevance and quantifiability, as characteristics of the good hypothesis. That is, a hypothesis should be as simple and concise as possible (while still explaining the facts), it should be relevant to the problem in the sense of providing a logically plausible solution, and it should ideally express the relationships between variables in the most precise form possible, i.e. in quantitative terms.

THE THEORETICAL AND METHODOLOGICAL APPROACH

What we have described so far are a set of *rules* for evaluating objectives and hypotheses. These rules are basically restrictive in the sense that they cut down the range of alternatives open to the researcher, but they do not actually provide positive guidance in the formulation of hypotheses or exploratory objectives. The major factor in guiding and suggesting solutions to research problems is the theoretical orientation which the scientist will have developed as a function of his reading, education, personality, and research experience. There are undoubtedly fashions in the type of theoretical framework that scientists tend to adopt, and there are indeed psychological theories about such fashions in theory,[8] but these need not concern us here. The point is simply that the fashions exist, and that they permeate the whole range of research decisions from the selection of the problem, through hypothesis formulation and research design, to the collection, analysis and interpretation of data.

Perhaps the most important dimension on which theoretical orientations differ is what might be described as the preferred *level of analysis;* that is, the degree of generality and abstraction implicit in the theory. Thus in sociology there are those who are interested in *grand theories,* who tend to develop global models of society and social change, and who tend to investigate *macro-topics* such as a cross-national study of the social effects of industrialisation. In contrast some sociologists prefer more specific levels of theorisation and study more molecular aspects of social life. For example the analysis of trends in social mobility may be conceptualised using a path model, in which father's occupation is held to influence son's education which in turn influences son's occupational achievement.

Psychologists are also confronted by a range of levels of analysis, and a corresponding range of research problems. Thus the psychologist who adopts a cybernetic model of human nature will tend to study fairly mechanical aspects of behaviour, such as the performance of skilled movements and reactions. Meanwhile those who analyse behaviour in terms of the way human beings structure their perceptions and place an emphasis on basic motivational factors are typically engaged in research into human relations, abnormal behaviour, socialisation and similar topics.

Related to the question of level of analysis is the degree of preference for quantitative or qualitative data. Thus as a general rule the more abstract theorists in the social sciences tend to argue for qualitative approaches, whereas those who adopt more molecular and specific theories are more likely to engage in precise, quantitative analysis. This is certainly true in psychology where, for example, the clinical psychologist tends to use qualitative research techniques such as the interview and case study, while the specialist in motor skills makes use of quantification and experimentation.

In addition to these variations in level of explanation and analysis there are, of course, competing conceptualisations *within* each level, so that the newcomer to the field is faced by a confusing array of different types of theoretical model often being applied to a single problem area. This theoretical 'pluralism' is usually regarded as the symptom of a young and developing science, and is not, in itself, unhealthy, since it serves to stimulate research and allows a wide range of tentative theories to be tested more or less simultaneously. Ultimately the relative progress of the different 'schools' of sociology and psychology is under the control of the scientific process which is continually assessing theoretical approaches in the light of empirical evidence. The choice of theoretical orientation must therefore remain a somewhat arbitrary matter until our empirical findings point more clearly to the strengths and weaknesses of the various approaches. Meanwhile we may note that many great social theorists including Marx, Weber and Durkheim made use of a wide range of conceptual models in developing their own contributions to social science.

Social scientists also differ in terms of the methodological framework in which they conduct their research, though here we can be more decisive about what constitutes an optimal choice. We have assumed in this book that the approach will be a scientific one, so that the effective choice is between two broad classes of research method which we have labelled *correlational* and *experimental*. The correlational methods make use of systematic observation of the relations between social variables which can be measured but not manipulated. This leads to a difficulty in testing causal hypotheses (see chapter 3). The experimental approach, in contrast, leads more definitely to the testing of causal relationships because the researcher is able to manipulate one variable and assess the corresponding changes in another variable while controlling other factors (see chapter 4). Of the two, the experimental approach is to be preferred for obvious reasons, but it is necessarily limited in its applications. Since the vast majority of the important social variables cannot be manipulated, the experimental method is used more rarely than the correlational alternatives—sample surveys, field studies and quasi-experimental designs. The main problem then is how to maximise the value of a correlational study for the purpose of testing specific hypotheses. As Moser[9] has pointed out, it is possible to get very close to the ideal of experimental control with a carefully designed survey, and in these circumstances one can be reasonably confident about the causal basis of the relationships obtained. He cites the research of Doll and Hill[10] on the relations between smoking and lung cancer as a model of how to maximise control of extraneous variables in a correlational design. Essentially the design consisted of a comparison between two matched groups of hospital patients one of which comprised cancer victims. The group members were individually matched on such variables as sex and age and the two groups were compared on various aspects of smoking habits. The observed relationship between smoking and cancer could not be ascribed to any of the variables controlled by matching and several other possible mediating factors were controlled by *measurement*, i.e. checking retrospectively that the groups did not differ on these factors. Thus it was difficult to imagine any factor other than smoking that could have caused the differences between the two groups. The only respect in which this study falls short of perfect experimental control is in its unavoidable failure to randomise the assignment of subjects to the groups. It is therefore theoretically possible, though not very likely, that some other extraneous variable which was not controlled by matching or measurement could have 'caused' both smoking and cancer. Thus by these relatively simple techniques it is possible to attain quite a good approximation to an experimental design. The use of correlational techniques to test causal hypotheses is now becoming increasingly popular with the development of more refined statistical techniques designed to 'extract' from one's data the effects of uncontrolled variables.

Hence even in a cross-sectional survey design it is sometimes possible to tease out the likely causal connections between variables using sophisticated statistical techniques such as multiple regression analyses.[11] The causal analysis of cross-sectional data in this way usually depends on some knowledge of the order in which the independent variables influenced the behaviour under study. If, in fact, a cross-sectional study can be repeated at two or more points in time, the possibility of determining which variables are influencing which is greatly increased. However this type of design is extremely difficult to analyse and appropriate statistical techniques are still in the process of development.[12]

A FINAL COMMENT

At this point in our discussion of strategy we come to the question of choosing the particular experimental or correlational design which will adequately test our theories or explore the social variables of interest. This is the subject matter of the book, and we hope that the preceding chapters will have helped the researcher in this task—both by outlining and evaluating the principal types of research design, and by specifying the assumptions underlying each one. But the rules of good research design cannot be specified precisely, as though one were programming a computer to handle the problem. There are inevitably points in the design process where decisions are based more on intuition than on rational analysis, and where the costs and payoffs cannot be sensibly predicted. It is sometimes difficult, for example, to decide between the descriptive richness of the case study and the representativeness of the sample survey, or between the simplicity of control by randomisation and the sensitivity of control by matching. We know in general terms the strengths and weaknesses of these different designs, and we can certainly relate this knowledge to our research aims, but there are cases where we may not always know whether a research problem will be more resistant to one mode of attack than another. It is here that judgment and experience take over from the more formal principles outlined in this book.

Research design then is both a technology and an art. Its purpose is to transform raw facts into evidence for or against a particular theory or hypothesis, and to the extent that it does this economically and validly it is 'good' research design. But it falls squarely within the *context of justification* (the formal process of assessing the truth value of theories) not within the *context of discovery*[13] (the creative process of generating new theories). We should not forget that the ultimate value of social research is determined by the product of the two.

References and further reading

CHAPTER 1.   EMPIRICISM IN THE SOCIAL SCIENCES

1. Alfred Schütz, 'Concept and theory formation in the social sciences', in D. Emmet and A. MacIntyre, eds, *Sociological Theory and Philosophical Analysis*, Macmillan; 1970, p. 2.

2. See James E. Curtis and John W. Petras, eds, *The Sociology of Knowledge: a reader*, Duckworth, 1970.

3. Alan Ryan, *The Philosophy of Social Sciences*, Macmillan, 1970, p. 65.

4. Ryan, p. 71f; Thomas S. Kuhn, *The Structure of Scientific Revolutions*, 2nd edn, Univ. of Chicago Press, 1970.

5. *Ibid.*

6. Other approaches to theory construction are sometimes proposed. For example *inductive theory* consists of a series of summary statements based on empirical findings. The object is to derive broad generalisations from the observed data rather than to use the data to test hypotheses set out before the investigation takes place. See, for example, W. C. Salmon, *The Foundations of Scientific Inference*, Univ. of Pittsburgh Press, 1966, p. 19.

7. Margaret Stacey, *Methods of Social Research*, Pergamon Press, 1969, p. 8.

8. P. F. Lazarsfeld and M. Rosenberg, eds, *The Language of Social Research*, Collier Macmillan, 1965, p. 184.

9. *Ibid.*, p. 75.

10. A variable is a property of something that can take on several different values, for example the *height* of males.

11. See H. M. Blalock, *Theory Construction : from verbal to mathematical formulation*, Prentice-Hall, 1969, p. 11.

12. R. M. MacIver, *Social Causation*, Harper Torchbooks, 1964, p. 385.

13. *Ibid.*

14. *Ibid.*, p. 386.

15. See R. K. Merton, 'The bearing of empirical research on sociological theory', in M. Brodbeck, ed, *Readings in the Philosophy of the Social Sciences,* Collier-Macmillan, 1968, p. 494.
16. See Michael Young, *Forecasting and the Social Sciences,* Heinemann, 1968, pp. 21–4.
17. *Ibid.,* p. 22.
18. MacIver, p. 26.

CHAPTER 2. MEASUREMENT

1. See Peter Chambers, *Techniques of Data Collection,* Longman (forthcoming).
2. P. W. Bridgman, *The Logic of Modern Physics,* Macmillan, 1928.
3. G. A. Lundberg, *Foundations of Sociology,* Macmillan, 1939.
4. S. S. Stevens, 'Psychology and the science of science', *Psychological Bulletin,* vol. 36, 1939, pp. 221–63.
5. H. M. Blalock, 'The measurement problem: a gap between the languages of theory and research', in H. M. Blalock and A. B. Blalock, eds, *Methodology in Social Research,* McGraw-Hill, 1968.
6. F. N. Kerlinger, *Foundations of Behavioural Research,* Holt, Rinehart & Winston, 1969, p. 35.
7. R. H. Waters and L. A. Pennington, 'Operationism in psychology', *Psychological Review,* vol. 45, 1938, pp. 414–23.
8. F. S. C. Northrop, *The Logic of the Sciences and the Humanities,* Macmillan, 1947, p. 127.
9. For a good account of the theory and measurement of *reliability* see: J. C. Nunnally, *Psychometric Theory,* McGraw-Hill, 1967.
10. This is because the differences between the scores of adjacent subjects are now much smaller and may be too small for the sensitivity of the measuring instrument. See Nunnally, p. 221 for computational details of correcting reliability coefficients for changes in dispersion of a set of scores.
11. For a more detailed discussion of testing main and auxiliary theories see Blalock and Blalock, pp. 19–27.
12. A good, non-mathematical introduction to factor analysis is presented by D. Child, *The Essentials of Factor Analysis,* Holt, Rinehart & Winston, 1970.
13. S. S. Stevens, 'On the theory of scales of measurement', *Science,* 1946, no. 103, pp. 677–80.
14. C. H. Coombs, 'Theory and methods of social measurement' in L. Festinger and D. Katz, eds, *Research Methods in the Behavioural Sciences,* Holt, Rinehart & Winston, 1953.

15. An excellent introductory text is provided by S. Siegal, *Non-Parametric Statistics for the Behavioural Sciences*, McGraw-Hill, 1956. More advanced developments are reviewed in E. Edgington, *Statistical Inference: the distribution-free approach*, McGraw-Hill, 1969.

16. See Nunnally, pp. 24–5.

17. Continuity and normality are statistical properties of variables. Continuity refers to the freedom of a variable to take on any value and not to be restricted to particular, finite values. Normality refers to the shape of the frequency distribution of a measure. Many psychological and social variables correspond very closely to the symmetrical, bell-shaped distribution which is known as the 'normal curve.

CHAPTER 3. FIELDWORK AND CORRELATIONAL DESIGNS

1. M. Zelditch, 'Some methodological problems of field studies', *American Journal of Sociology*, vol. 67 (1962).

2. 'Universe' may be defined as 'the aggregate of units to which the survey results are to apply', see C. A. Moser and G. Kalton, *Survey Methods in Social Investigation*, 2nd edn, Heinemann Educational, 1971, p. 53.

3. Norman K. Denzin, *Sociological Methods: a sourcebook*, Butterworths, 1970, p. 117.

4. *Ibid;* see also Norman K. Denzin, *The Research Act in Sociology*, Butterworths, 1970, pp. 89–96.

5. Moser and Kalton, chapters 5 and 6.

6. *Ibid.*, p. 80.

7. L. Kish, *Survey Sampling*, Wiley, 1965.

8. Related to the above designs is *area sampling* defined as 'multi-stage sampling in which maps rather than lists or registers, serve as the sampling frame'; see Moser and Kalton, p. 118.

9. Controlling for age and sex independently could easily destroy representativeness in that for instance if 50 per cent each of males and females are chosen without reference to their age distribution in the population, the males may contain far fewer middle-aged people than this age cohort has in fact in the population. Interrelating the controls means that within each sex group the correct proportions of each age cohort are included. Interrelating the controls becomes much more complex than this when half-a-dozen variables are used.

10. Another problem exists due to the fact that information about refusals is usually not available.

11. W. D. Wall and H. L. Williams, *Longitudinal Studies and the Social Sciences,* Heinemann for the SSRC, 1970, p. 8.

12. *Ibid.,* p. 9.

13. *Ibid.,* p. 22.

14. *Ibid.,* p. 20.

15. G. C. Helmstadter, *Research Concepts in Human Behaviour: education, psychology, sociology,* Appleton-Century-Crofts, 1970, pp. 83–6.

16. See Margaret Stacey, *Methods of Social Research,* Pergamon Press, 1969, p. 64.

17. For a brief discussion of problems of time-sampling see Johan Galtung, *Theory and Methods of Social Research,* Allen & Unwin, 1967, pp. 23ff, 65ff.

18. See 1 per cent sample, 1971 Census.

19. For a discussion of content analysis see W. J. Goode and P. K. Hatt, *Methods in Social Research,* McGraw-Hill, 1952, pp. 325–30.

20. For example a 'census' of 1 per cent of households was started in March 1972, to find out details about incomes. This enquiry was based on the voluntary cooperation of the individuals in the sample chosen, see *The Guardian,* 22 March 1972.

21. Complete enumeration is an ideal which is never quite attained.

22. In the 1971 Census for England and Wales, the country was split into 106,173 enumeration districts, which were covered by 96,741 enumerators. The average number of households in urban areas was 150 but in some more sparsely populated rural areas enumeration districts contained as few as 70 households.

23. B. Benjamin, *Demographic Analysis*, Allen & Unwin, 1968, p. 23.

24. See Elizabeth Colson, 'The intensive study of small sample communities' in A. L. Epstein, ed, *The Craft of Social Anthropology,* Tavistock, 1967, p. 11.

25. See J. P. Dean, R. L. Eichhorn and L. R. Dean, 'Limitations and advantages of unstructured methods' in G. J. McCall and J. L. Simmons, eds, *Issues in Participant Observation,* Addison-Wesley, 1969, p. 20.

26. N. K. Denzin, *The Research Act in Sociology,* Butterworths, 1970, p. 186.

27. J. Galtung, p. 68.

28. See B. Berelson, 'Content analysis', in G. Lindzey, ed., *Handbook of Social Psychology,* Addison-Wesley, 1954, p. 489.

29. Eugene J. Webb, *et al., Unobtrusive Measures : non-reactive research in the social sciences,* Rand McNally, Chicago, 1966, p. 53.
30. B. R. Wilson, 'Analytical studies of social institutions' in Welford *et al.,* eds, *Society,* pp. 99–110.
31. W. J. Goode and P. K. Hatt, *Methods in Social Research,* McGraw-Hill, 1952, p. 133.
32. We do not consider here 'depth interviewing', which is the most flexible approach and a highly specialised technique. This is not within the purview of this book.
33. A. N. Oppenheim, *Questionnaire Design and Attitude Measurement,* Heinemann, 1966, see especially chapters 2,3,5 and 6.
34. A *leading question* may be defined as 'one which, by its content, structure or wording, leads the respondent in the direction of a certain answer', see Moser and Kalton, p. 323.
35. Oppenheim, p. 60. Split-ballot trials, i.e. where surveys are randomly divided into two or more segments running simultaneously under identical conditions, the only variation being the form of the questionnaire used in each segment, show that results are influenced not only by the particular wording but also by the general design of questionnaires; see Elisabeth Noelle-Neumann, 'Wanted: rules for wording structured questionnaires', *Political Opinion Quarterly,* vol. 34, 1970.
36. See E. Krausz, *Sociology in Britain : a survey of research,* Batsford, 1969, p. 72.
37. See R. K. Merton, M. Fiske and P. L. Kendall, *The Focused Interview,* New York, Free Press, 1956, especially chapters 1 and 8.
38. *Ibid.,* pp. 12, 15f.
39. *Ibid.,* p. 16f.
40. *Ibid.,* p. 4.
41. *Ibid.,* pp. 178ff.
42. See James A. Davis, *Elementary Survey Analysis,* Prentice-Hall, 1971, p. 50f.
43. Moser and Kalton, pp. 47–51.
44. Stein Rokkan, 'Cross-cultural, cross-societal and cross-national research' in *Main trends of research in the social and human sciences,* Paris, UNESCO, and The Hague, Mouton, 1970, p. 646.
45. See P. Kendall and P. F. Lazarsfeld, 'Problems of survey analysis' in R. K. Merton and P. F. Lazarsfeld, eds, *Continuities in Social Research,* New York, Free Press, 1950, pp. 133–96; see also Rokkan, p. 652.

46. Rokkan, p. 654.
47. *Ibid.*
48. *Ibid.*
49. Galtung, pp. 437–50.
50. Margaret Stacey, ed, *Comparability in Social Research,* Heinemann for SSRC/BSA, 1969.
51. *Ibid.,* p. 13.
52. See *Report of Annual General Meeting,* British Sociological Association, 12 April 1972, p. 1.
53. Frank Bechhofer, 'Occupation', in Stacey, p. 118.
54. Ernest Krausz, 'Religion as a key variable', in Elizabeth Gittus, ed, *Key Variables in Social Research,* vol. 1, Heinemann for BSA, 1972, ch. 1.
55. Gittus, Introduction.

CHAPTER 4.   EXPERIMENTAL METHODS

1. J. S. Bruner and C. C. Goodman, 'Value and need as organizing factors in perception', *Journal of Abnormal Social Psychology,* vol. 42, 1947, pp. 33–44.
2. W. Ashley, R. Harper, and D. Runyon, 'The perceived size of coins in normal and hypnotically induced economic states', *American Journal of Psychology,* vol. 64, 1951, pp. 564–72.
3. A full explanation of the purpose and design of such experiments should always be offered at the completion of the research. In addition careful thought should be given to the ethical design of such experiments (see Symposium Report on Ethical Problems in Psychology, *British Psychological Society Bulletin,* May 1972). For a detailed discussion of techniques for avoiding artificial behaviour in experiments see J. Ross and P. Smith, 'Orthodox experimental designs', in H. Blalock and A. B. Blalock, eds, *Methodology in Social Research,* McGraw-Hill, 1968.
4. Harold Leavitt, 'Some effects of certain communication patterns on group performance', *Journal of Abnormal and Social Psychology,* vol. 46, 1951, 38–50.
5. F. J. McGuigan, *Experimental Psychology,* 2nd edn, Prentice-Hall, 1968, p. 58.
6. N. Morse, 'An experimental study in an industrial organisation', in H. Guetzkow, ed, *Groups, Leadership and Men,* Carnegie Press, 1951, pp. 96–9.

7. Ross and Smith, *op.cit.*

8. J. P. French, 'Experiments in field settings' in Festinger and Katz eds, *Research Methods in the Behavioural Sciences,* Holt, Rinehart and Winston, 1953, chapter 3.

9. An excellent survey of experimental designs is given by W. G. Cochran and G. N. Cox, *Experimental Designs,* 2nd edn, Wiley, 1957. For statistical procedures see B. J. Winer, *Statistical Principles in Experimental Design,* McGraw-Hill, 1962.

10. Ross and Smith, pp. 370ff.

11. For example a trend test, see Winer.

12. These additional analyses are known as tests of paired comparisons; see Winer.

13. This principle can be easily extended to factorial designs.

14. One can be much more precise about when to use a matched-groups design in preference to a randomised design. The answer depends on the correlation between the matching variable and the dependent variable, and also on the number of subjects. It is also possible to compute the optimal number of matching levels for any particular design. See Jerome L. Myers, *Fundamentals of Experimental Design*, Allyn & Bacon, Boston, 1966, pp. 139–46.

15. See Winer for details.

16. See J. Wiggins, 'Hypothesis validity and experimental laboratory methods', in Blalock and Blalock, for a detailed analysis of experimenter effects.

CHAPTER 5. STRATEGY AND CHOICE

1. H. Winthrop, 'Cultural determinants of psychological research values', *Journal of Social Psychology,* vol. 53, 1961, pp. 255–69.

2. W. B. Webb, 'The choice of problem', *American Psychologist,* vol. 16, 1961, 223–7.

3. F. N. Kerlinger, *Foundations of Behavioural Research,* Holt, Rinehart & Winston, 1969, p. 13.

4. H. Hyman, *Survey Design and Analysis,* Collier-Macmillan, 1967, p. 68.

5. See Peter Blau, 'The research process in the study of dynamics of bureaucracy', in Phillip E. Hammond, ed. *Sociologists at Work: essays in the craft of social research,* New York, Basic Books, 1964, p. 20.

6. See Hyman, p. 85.

Name Index

Subject Index